easy vegetable meals

easy
vegetable meals

A Fuss-Free Cookbook for Everyone

Larissa Olczak

Photography by Emulsion Studio

ROCKRIDGE
PRESS

Interior and Cover Designer: Richard Tapp
Art Producer: Sue Bischofberger
Editor: Erum Khan
Production Manager: Jose Olivera
Production Editor: Melissa Edeburn
Photography © 2020 Emulsion Studio.
Front Cover: Jap Chae Vegetable Medley, p. 43; Back Cover: Orange-Pomegranate Salsa, p. 144; Cauliflower Crust Veggie Pizza, p.127; Winter Harvest Quinoa Stir-Fry, p. 137
ISBN: Print 978-1-64611-513-6 | eBook 978-1-64611-514-3
R0

I would like to dedicate this book to my amazing mom, who has been nothing but loving and supportive throughout my life.

CONTENTS

**WINTER HARVEST
QUINOA STIR-FRY,**
PAGE 137

INTRODUCTION

Eating lots of vegetables every day can seem daunting, but it doesn't have to be. This cookbook will help you make the most of the veggies available at your local grocery store, seasonal farm-to-table food delivery service, food co-op, and farmers' market while speaking to your real challenge: a dearth of time for preparing nutritious meals. In recognition of that challenge, I've filled this book with meals that take less than 30 minutes to prepare, require only one pot to make, or use no more than five main ingredients.

The recipes in each chapter progress from lighter to heavier meals. Sometimes we need a warm, heavy root vegetable stew. Other times a light veggie-packed spring roll is perfectly satisfying.One chapter is devoted to my favorite way to spice up a meal: plant-based sauces! These sauces go great with the recipes in this book. Moreover, you can use them to incorporate veggies into your own creations.

I have been enjoying a vegetarian diet for more than a decade and have spent countless hours in the kitchen experimenting with creative ways to make vegetable dishes simple and delicious. As a nutritional therapy practitioner (NTP), I have seen how eating vegetables has helped people feel amazing and overcome a variety of health conditions. Eating more vegetables benefits everyone. Whether you are a strict vegan, a vegetarian simply looking for inspiration in the kitchen, or an omnivore trying to add more plants to your plate, I've got your back. Throughout these chapters, I'll teach you multiple ways to prepare vegetables and give you tips on how to incorporate meat or make meals vegan.

I'm thrilled to show you creative ways to cook tasty veggie meals for every season of the year. Soon you'll be a vegetable-cooking pro!

chapter one
vegetable cooking essentials

Welcome to the beginning of your journey to eating more vegetables. In this chapter, we'll go over some tips and tricks for sourcing produce, stocking your pantry, and prepping and cooking vegetables. I'm excited to show you how to create tasty, healthy, and easy-to-make dishes.
Let's get started!

So, You Want to Eat More Veggies

Vegetables are often limited to side salads, and they have a reputation for being bland. I'm here to show you how to easily create delicious meals featuring vegetables. With the right cooking methods and seasonings, you can use vegetables to make satisfying main dishes that you'll want to eat again and again.

WHERE TO BUY YOUR PRODUCE

Many of us buy our vegetables and fruit at the grocery store, but there are many more options for finding fresh, seasonal produce. These include:

Community-supported agriculture (CSA) programs put the consumer directly in touch with local farms. Consumers pay a monthly, seasonal, or annual fee for a "share," a portion of a farm's harvest. This share might include fresh, seasonal vegetables and fruit, but can also extend to eggs and even meat. CSA programs create relationships between consumers and farmers, shine a light on the source and production of food, and support local businesses. Search online to find a CSA near you.

Farmers' markets are another great way to support the local economy and farmers while also getting fresh, seasonal produce. Farmers bring their fresh produce to a central location for consumers to browse and purchase. Farmers' markets are usually scheduled on weekends, but some operate on weekdays as well. Check your local paper or search online to find days and times for farmers' markets in your area.

Online grocery shopping has been gaining momentum over the past several years. Some of my favorite online grocery stores are Thrive-Market.com, Instacart, and Amazon Fresh. Most standard grocery stores now have an online option, too.

In-season produce generally tastes better than the same fruit or vegetable purchased out of season. There are a lot of compelling reasons to eat (and cook) with the seasons.

It's More Cost-Effective. Seasonal produce is cheaper to produce, harvest, and distribute than nonseasonal produce. As a result, seasonal produce is generally less expensive for us to buy.

It's Nutrient Dense. Eating seasonal produce fuels your body with the vitamins, minerals, and antioxidants needed during that specific time of year.

It's Fresh. Seasonal produce is fresh and vibrant because it grows in your region. Nonseasonal produce may be coated with wax or treated with preservatives to make it last past its peak. On its journey to your plate, imported produce may lose nutrition, and transporting it contributes to air and water pollution.

You Support Local Farmers. Farmers work hard to produce food to nourish you and your family. Eating locally and seasonally helps your local farms thrive.

Is Organic Really Better?

What makes a food product "USDA certified organic"? That label means the product has met certain standards. Namely, it contains no GMOs (genetically modified organisms) and it has been grown without the use of synthetic pesticides, herbicides, or fungicides. Keep in mind that a non-GMO label does *not* indicate that the product is organic.

Every year, the Environmental Working Group (EWG) publishes two lists: the Clean Fifteen and the Dirty Dozen. These lists advise consumers on which produce should be purchased as organic. The Clean Fifteen are 15 fruits and vegetables that tested lowest for pesticides—in short, it's safe to purchase conventional varieties of this produce. The Dirty Dozen are the 12 fruits and vegetables that tested highest for pesticides and should be purchased organic when possible.

It's okay if you can't find organic vegetables. Vegetables in *general* are packed with important antioxidants, vitamins, and minerals that our bodies need. Soak nonorganic produce in a mixture of 5 to 7 cups water and ¼ cup apple cider vinegar or baking soda. This wash will remove unwanted residues and any adhesives.

Labels can be helpful when you are purchasing nonproduce groceries. Look for meat and eggs labeled "grass-fed," "pasture-raised," "antibiotic-free," and "hormone-free."

Fresh versus Frozen

It's not always possible to get fresh, seasonal produce. That's okay! There are other options. You can preserve vegetables from the market or your own garden by blanching and freezing them until frozen solid (about 2 hours). Transfer them to an airtight container and store them in your freezer, where they will keep for 6 months or more.

Buying frozen vegetables is also a great option. Vegetables are frozen at their peak of freshness, preserving their nutritional value and flavor, so you don't have to worry about missing out on healthy vitamins and minerals.

What You'll Need in the Kitchen

You'll want to keep a handful of tools and ingredients in your kitchen to make the recipes in this book.

EQUIPMENT AND TOOLS

MUST-HAVES

Large Stainless-Steel Pot and Skillet: A good pot and skillet are essential for making one-pot meals. You need plenty of space for water and vegetables. Most of the recipes in this book require one large pot and one large skillet.

Blender: I love using my blender to make veggie soups in the winter and sauces in the summer. You can also use the pulse function on a blender for chopping and mixing the ingredients for some recipes.

Large Wooden Cutting Board: You'll need plenty of room for prepping vegetables.

Vegetable Peeler: A peeler makes it easy to prep vegetables and fruit like apples, winter squash, beets, and potatoes. To make cleanup easy, peel produce over a large bowl or the wastebasket.

NICE-TO-HAVES

Cast-Iron Skillet: A cast-iron skillet is a multifunction pan. You can use it on the stovetop for sautéing and searing, and in the oven for baking dishes like quiches and frittatas, as well as breads and desserts like cobblers. A cast-iron skillet is also a great way to get extra iron in your diet.

Spiralizer Use this tool to replace grain-based noodles with veggie "noodles."

Baking Sheet: A baking sheet is essential for baking or roasting vegetables.

Wok: Woks heat up quickly and are great for stir-frying rice and noodle dishes.

Garlic Press: A garlic press makes it easy to prep garlic for a recipe. After you press garlic, let it stand for 7 minutes before adding it to the dish to increase the amount of allicin, a beneficial nutrient.

KITCHEN STAPLES

Olive Oil: Olive oil is probably the ingredient I use most in my kitchen. It's included in most of the recipes in this book, and it's full of antioxidants. Avoid canola oil and other vegetable oils, which oxidize easily and can cause inflammation. Grass-fed butter and ghee are also healthy and good to have on hand.

Himalayan Pink Salt: Unlike regular table salt, Himalayan pink salt is loaded with 84 essential minerals, and it's far more nutritious.

Turmeric: This beautiful yellow spice boasts many health benefits. Pairing turmeric with black pepper and a fat like olive oil or ghee makes the healing and anti-inflammatory properties of the spice more bioavailable.

Beans: Canned or dried beans are a staple in many of the dishes in this book. Beans are full of protein, which is vital to maintaining healthy muscles. You can store dried beans in jars or other glass containers. When buying canned beans, opt for low-sodium varieties packaged in cans with BPA-free linings.

Nutritional Yeast: Packed with B vitamins, nutritional yeast is a must for the kitchen. It gives food a delicious cheesy flavor.

Vegetable Broth or Miso Paste: Both vegetable broth and miso paste are great ways to add extra flavor to dishes and to build flavor in soups.

Leafy Greens: I always have some sort of seasonal greens in my refrigerator. Leafy greens are packed with health-boosting vitamins, minerals, fiber, and antioxidants. They feed the good bacteria in our gut and boost our immune system. It's easy to incorporate greens into practically any dish.

Grains: Grains such as rice, quinoa, and barley are pantry staples that offer a tasty and convenient way to turn simple veggie sides into complete meals.

Cooking for Different Diets

Cooking for multiple dietary needs under one roof can be difficult, but it's not impossible. In this book, you will find recipes to please meat eaters, vegetarians, and vegans alike. I've included substitutions to make recipes dairy free, gluten free, and nut free, so you can cook for everyone. Following is a list of ingredients you can use to replace animal products in recipes to better address your or your family's dietary needs without compromising flavor.

- **Beans and legumes.** Beans and legumes like lentils are excellent sources of protein. Pair beans with rice to form a complete protein.
- **Coconut cream.** Coconut cream is a thicker and sweeter nondairy milk. It contains more fat, so it's great to use in seasonal curries and baked goods.
- **Coconut oil.** Coconut oil can be used as a replacement for butter in many recipes. It contains essential fatty acids, and its slightly sweet flavor makes foods taste delicious.

- **Flaxseed meal.** Combining flaxseed meal (ground flax-seed) with water activates compounds in the flaxseed that cause the mixture to gel and develop an egglike consistency, so it's a handy replacement for eggs in baked goods. To make a "flax egg" equivalent to 1 large egg, in a small bowl, stir together 1 tablespoon flaxseed meal and 3 tablespoons water and let stand for 5 minutes before using. (If your recipe calls for more than one egg, just double or triple the quantities of flaxseed meal and water as needed.)
- **Mushrooms.** Mushrooms have a similar amino acid profile to meat, as well as a meaty texture, so they can be used in recipes to replace meat but retain the dish's flavor profile and consistency. Combine mushrooms with broccoli and corn to create a complete protein.
- **Nondairy milks.** Similar to dairy milk in consistency and appearance, milks made from plant-based ingredients like oats, almonds, or cashews are a great replacement for dairy in most recipes or can be enjoyed on their own.
- **Tofu.** A great source of protein, tofu leaves you feeling full and satisfied. Tofu can replace cheese, eggs, or meat in many dishes.

Vegetable Prep Basics

Prepping vegetables might seem tedious and time-consuming. However, with the right prep station and tools, you can accomplish this task quickly and easily. For more instructions on prepping and cooking specific ingredients, check out the reference guide on page 151. When chopping or slicing vegetables or other produce, use a sharp chef's knife; use a sharp paring knife for tasks like trimming ingredients or cutting out bruised spots. Knowing a few basic knife cuts can help you easily break down whole vegetables.

Dice. To dice an ingredient means to cut it into uniform cubes or pieces (a recipe will usually tell you what size those pieces should be).

Cutting ingredients to a uniform size means each piece will cook at the same rate, which is especially useful when you're making dishes like soups and stir-fries. Start by slicing off one end of the vegetable to give yourself a flat surface to place against your cutting board to keep the vegetable stable as you continue dicing. For round or roundish ingredients like potatoes and beets, you can cut a slice from any side; for longer tapered vegetables like carrots and parsnips, either cut a slice lengthwise along the rounded side or cut off the root end. Stand the vegetable on your cutting board and cut it into equal pieces that are as wide as the dice size specified in the recipe. Stack the slices (or a few slices at a time, for larger vegetables) and cut them into equal sticks with the same width as the slices. Finally, turn the sticks horizontally and cut across them into uniform cubes.

Julienne. To julienne an ingredient means to cut it into skinny matchsticks. Use the same technique as for dicing, but cut slices about 1/8 inch thick, and cut the sticks into 2- to 3-inch lengths instead of cubes.

Chiffonade. If you want to cut leafy ingredients like greens or herbs into uniform shreds, use a technique called chiffonade. Stack the leaves on top of one another. Roll them into a cylinder, then slice the cylinder crosswise to form strips.

Mince. To mince is to cut into very small pieces. It's a great technique to use with ingredients like garlic and ginger because you can evenly disperse the flavor throughout a dish. Use the same method as for dicing, but make your slices very thin. You don't have to create perfect cubes or equal-size pieces; just be sure you don't leave any large chunks.

Basic Cooking Techniques

Vegetables are versatile and packed with flavor, and they usually don't require much cooking time. Here are some of the easiest ways to cook them.

Steaming. Fill a large pot with 2 to 3 inches of water and set a steamer basket in the pot. Bring the water to a simmer over high heat, then reduce the heat to maintain a simmer. Put the veggies in the steamer basket, cover the pot, and cook until the veggies are tender or as directed in the recipe. The cooking time will depend on the type of vegetable and the size of the pieces (if you have prepped). Veggies like broccoli, cauliflower, and greens require less cooking time than potatoes, sweet potatoes, carrots, and winter squash. Season steamed vegetables with a little bit of lemon juice and ground mustard seed to add back up to 40 percent of the nutrients lost during steaming.

Roasting. Roasting vegetables is one of my favorite ways to prepare them. Preheat the oven to between 400° and 450°F. Grease a baking sheet with ghee or avocado oil. Spread chopped or smaller whole vegetables (such as baby potatoes or Brussels sprouts) evenly over the prepared pan, leaving some space between them (packing them too close together will cause them to steam instead of roast). Roast for 25 to 30 minutes, until golden brown and tender, or as directed in the recipe.

Sautéing. In a skillet, heat the cooking oil of your choice over medium heat. When the oil is hot, add prepped or small whole veggies such as peas and cook, stirring, until soft (or translucent, for ingredients like onions).

Boiling. Boiling is a great option for vegetables being used in a soup, because the nutrient-dense broth will replace the vitamins and minerals lost during boiling. Fill a large pot with water to about 3 inches below the top of the pot. Bring the water to a boil over high heat. Add the vegetables and reduce the heat to maintain a simmer. Cover and cook until tender or as directed in the recipe. The cooking time will vary depending on the ingredient, anywhere from 15 to 20 minutes for starchier vegetables like potatoes, to 5 to 10 minutes for vegetables such as carrots, cauliflower, and broccoli, and as little as 3 to 5 minutes for peas.

Grilling. Heat an outdoor grill to the heat level called for in the recipe. When the grill is hot, oil the grill grates, then place the veggies on the grill. (Alternatively, heat a grill pan over medium-high heat, then coat the pan with oil and add the veggies.) Cook for the time specified in the recipe (with the lid open or closed as specified), then flip the vegetables and grill as directed. Avoid flipping the vegetables more than once.

Common Flavor Combinations

Here are some of my favorite flavor combinations to add flavor to almost any vegetable.

- **Olive oil + lemon juice + rosemary + salt + pepper:** This savory flavor combination is great on mushrooms, fish, and potatoes.
- **Nutritional yeast + salt:** Nutritional yeast has a cheesy flavor and is packed with important B vitamins. Use this combination for noodles or in dishes that typically call for cheese.
- **Black salt:** This type of salt contains a lot of sulfur, which gives it a strong and delicious eggy flavor.
- **Soy sauce + brown sugar:** A sweet-and-savory teriyaki-like combination great for stir-fries and fried rice. You can use coconut aminos instead of soy sauce if you prefer.
- **Sriracha + soy sauce + toasted sesame oil:** A spicy, nutty, and savory flavor for homemade sushi or rice bowls.
- **Fish sauce + brown sugar + lime or lemon juice:** This combination is great for rice or noodle dishes and can also be used as a dip or marinade. Add chopped Thai chiles for a kick of heat.

- **Honey + Dijon mustard + cayenne pepper + smoked paprika:** Use this combination as a sweet-and-spicy marinade for fish or vegetables.
- **Plain Greek yogurt + lemon juice + dill:** A great cooling sauce to use on beans, falafel, or sandwiches.
- **Tomato + basil + olive oil + salt:** An amazing and authentic Italian flavor combination for spaghetti or sandwiches.
- **Avocado + mango + lemon juice + salt:** This sweet, sour, and salty combination is like a quick guacamole and makes a great addition to fish dishes such as fish tacos; it also tastes great with a grilled cauliflower steak.

About These Easy Meals

The recipes in this book will make it easier than ever for you to introduce more veggies into your diet. Some recipes use no more than five main ingredients (not including oil, salt, and pepper). Others take no more than 30 minutes to prepare, or require just one pot or pan. Each recipe will be clearly marked with one or more of these labels, so you can choose which dish you'd like to make based on your ingredients, how much time you have to cook, or how many dishes you feel like cleaning up afterward.

Each recipe is adaptable to suit any dietary preference and includes substitutions for common allergens. While the majority of the recipes are vegetarian, some do use meat, but I've included alternative ingredients to make these dishes suitable for meat eaters *and* vegans alike.

The chapters are organized by season—starting with spring, summer, fall, and finally winter—to help keep flavor up and cost down. Each chapter starts with lighter meals that make good breakfasts or lunches and moves on to heavier dinners.

My goal is to provide you with convenient and tasty veggie-based recipes that you will make over and over again. And whether you are cooking for yourself or for your family, this book has something for everyone to enjoy.

RISOTTO WITH
ASPARAGUS AND
SNAP PEAS
PAGE 29

2

chapter two **spring**
March Through May

Spring is the season for avocados, asparagus, mushrooms, onions, peas, and greens like kale, collards, and spinach.

Spring Onion Soup

DAIRY-FREE, NUT-FREE, VEGETARIAN

This flavorful soup is light and delicious for warm weather. Onions are packed with vitamins and minerals, such as vitamin C and potassium, making this soup very nutritious. Try adding fresh or frozen snap peas for a pop of color and sweetness. The cheesy bread also adds a delicious crunch.

Serves 3   **Prep time: 15 minutes / Cook time: 55 minutes**

¼ cup olive oil

5 yellow onions, sliced

3 garlic cloves

2 teaspoons dried thyme

¾ cup red wine

3 tablespoons all-purpose flour or gluten-free flour

8 cups vegetable broth

2 teaspoons sea salt, plus more for seasoning

2 teaspoons freshly ground black pepper, plus more for seasoning

3 ounces peas

½ baguette, sliced

4 ounces mozzarella cheese (optional)

1. In a large pot, heat the olive oil over low heat. Add the onions and cook, stirring often, for 20 to 25 minutes, until they are translucent and very soft.

2. Add the garlic and thyme and cook, stirring, for 1 minute.

3. Slowly pour in the wine. Increase the heat to medium to bring to a simmer, then reduce the heat to low and simmer for 10 minutes, or until the wine has evaporated.

4. Add the flour and cook, stirring continuously, for 1 minute.

5. Slowly pour in the broth, then add the salt and pepper. Increase the heat to medium-high. Bring the soup to a boil, then reduce the heat to maintain a simmer and cook for 15 minutes.

6. Taste the soup and season with salt and pepper. Top with the peas.

7. In a small bowl, ladle in the soup until half full. Add sliced bread and continue ladling in the soup. Top with mozzarella cheese, if using. Serve immediately.

Substitution Tip: You can use beef or chicken broth instead of vegetable broth.

PER SERVING: Calories: 491; Total fat: 18g; Total carbs: 61g; Fiber: 7g; Sugar: 13g; Protein: 10g; Sodium: 1,912mg

Tangy Veggie Skewers

DAIRY-FREE, GLUTEN-FREE, NUT-FREE, VEGAN

You can make this easy, flexible spring recipe with the vegetables you have in your refrigerator. You can also easily incorporate meat, which is a great option for a barbecue or picnic. For a different spin, serve the baked vegetables in a corn tortilla for delicious tacos.

Serves 4 **Prep time: 20 minutes / Cook time: 25 minutes**

3 red onions, quartered

3 zucchini, cut into 1-inch-thick slices

2 red bell peppers, cut into 1-inch-wide slices

2 orange bell peppers, cut into 1-inch-wide slices

2 yellow bell peppers, cut into 1-inch-wide slices

2 portabella mushrooms, cut into 1-inch-thick slices

Olive oil

Salt

Freshly ground black pepper

1. Soak wooden skewers in water to cover for 15 minutes, then drain.

2. Preheat the oven to 375°F.

3. Skewer the vegetables, starting with onion, then zucchini, bell peppers, mushrooms, and onion again. Drizzle the skewers with olive oil, season with salt and pepper, and place the skewers on a baking sheet. Bake for 25 minutes.

4. Serve immediately. You can store leftovers in an airtight container in the refrigerator for up to 2 days.

Prep Tip: Prep your vegetables while your skewers soak. Try to make all the pieces relatively the same size. When threading the skewers, leave some space between the vegetables so there is room for air to circulate.

Substitution Tip: If you like, you can add pieces of meat after the first onion and after the mushroom.

PER SERVING: Calories: 229; Total fat: 12g; Total carbs: 31g; Fiber: 6g; Sugar: 9g; Protein: 7g; Sodium: 64mg

Glazed Tofu Lettuce Cups

DAIRY-FREE, VEGAN

This quick and refreshing dish is filling and nourishing. It will satisfy all your flavor cravings, from salty to sweet to sour—you can even make it spicy! Tofu is a good source of protein, and carrots are rich in beta-carotene, fiber, vitamin K, and antioxidants.

Serves 4   **Prep time: 15 minutes / Cook time: 20 minutes**

1 (14-ounce) package
   rice noodles
½ cup peanut butter
2 tablespoons soy sauce
1 tablespoon sesame oil
1 tablespoon rice vinegar
1 tablespoon maple syrup
1 (14-ounce) block
   extra-firm tofu, cubed
4 butter lettuce leaves
1 bunch fresh
   cilantro, chopped

1. Cook the rice noodles according to the package instructions. Drain and let cool.

2. In a small bowl, stir together the peanut butter, soy sauce, sesame oil, vinegar, and maple syrup until smooth.

3. In a large nonstick skillet, cook the tofu over medium heat for 5 minutes. With a spatula or wooden spoon, stir the tofu cubes, then cook for 5 minutes more, until brown and crispy.

4. Add the sauce to the pan and stir to coat the tofu, then cook for 3 minutes. Remove from the heat.

5. Place a lettuce leaf on each of four plates. Divide the noodles among the lettuce leaves, then top with the tofu mixture and the cilantro. Serve immediately.

Substitution Tip: If you prefer to add meat to this recipe, you can replace the tofu with chicken.

PER SERVING: Calories: 563; Total fat: 27g; Total carbs: 60g; Fiber: 4g; Sugar: 7g; Protein: 21g; Sodium: 709mg

Spring Loaded Nachos

NUT-FREE, ONE POT, 30-MINUTE, VEGETARIAN

Nachos may sound like a snack, but done the right way, they can be a simple, convenient, and delicious meal. Throw together the ingredients on a baking sheet or in a skillet, bake for a few minutes, and you're done. Bonus? You can use any vegetables you already have in your kitchen.

Serves 4   **Prep time: 15 minutes / Cook time: 10 minutes**

**1 (12-ounce) bag
  tortilla chips**
**1 (15-ounce) can black
  beans, drained
  and rinsed**
**½ cup shredded
  Cheddar cheese**
1 red onion, chopped
**1 head romaine lettuce,
  shredded**
**1 avocado, pitted, peeled,
  and cubed**

1. Preheat the oven to 400°F.

2. Place the tortilla chips in a baking dish or oven-safe skillet.

3. Top the chips with the black beans, cheese, and onion.

4. Bake for 5 to 10 minutes. Remove from the oven.

5. Top the nachos with the lettuce and avocado and serve.

Prep Tip: Start checking on the nachos at 3 minutes. You want the cheese to melt, but be careful the chips don't burn.

Substitution Tip: To make this recipe vegan friendly, replace the Cheddar cheese with store-bought vegan cheese, or use the Spicy Cashew Cheese on page 143.

PER SERVING: Calories: 652; Total fat: 32g; Total carbs: 80g; Fiber: 14g; Sugar: 3g; Protein: 17g; Sodium: 455mg

Rainbow Collard Green Wrap

DAIRY-FREE, GLUTEN-FREE, NUT-FREE, 30-MINUTE, VEGAN

Antioxidants give fruits and vegetables their beautiful colors, and this wrap is filled with them. The hummus and tofu add extra protein, and the rice noodles leave you feeling full.

Serves 4   **Prep time: 15 minutes / Cook time: 10 minutes**

1 (14-ounce) package thin rice noodles
4 large collard leaves
½ cup prepared hummus
½ (14-ounce) block tofu, sliced
1 carrot, cut into thin matchsticks
1 yellow bell pepper, cut into thin strips
1 cucumber, cut into thin strips
¼ head purple cabbage, shredded

1. Cook the rice noodles according to the package instructions. Drain.

2. Run the collard leaves under cold water and lay them on paper towels to dry.

3. Lay the collard leaves on your cutting board. Top the middle of each leaf with 2 tablespoons of hummus. Divide the noodles evenly among the collard leaves, followed by the tofu, carrot, bell pepper, cucumber, and cabbage.

4. Roll each collard leaf from the top toward the stem, tucking in the filling as you go. Cut each wrap in half with a sharp knife and serve immediately.

Prep Tip: If the collard leaves are too tough, very quickly blanch them in boiling water and then submerge them in ice water for 1 minute or run under cold water for 1 minute to stop the cooking.

PER SERVING: Calories: 384; Total fat: 9g; Total carbs: 62g; Fiber: 9g; Sugar: 5g; Protein: 16g; Sodium: 189mg

Zesty Mushroom Carnitas

The texture and flavors of this hearty mushroom dish will satisfy both vegans and meat eaters. Pull the mushrooms apart so they have a consistency like pulled pork. You can enjoy them alone, with brown rice, or even in tacos. Make this dish gluten free by using coconut aminos instead of soy sauce.

Serves 2   **Prep time: 10 minutes / Cook time: 20 minutes**

1 onion, sliced

3 garlic cloves, minced

3 tablespoons soy sauce
or coconut aminos

2 teaspoons
dried oregano

1 teaspoon ground cumin

¼ teaspoon freshly
ground black pepper

2 teaspoons
smoked paprika

2 teaspoons freshly
squeezed lime juice,
plus more for serving

12 cremini or portabella
mushrooms, sliced

2 tablespoons olive oil

4 corn tortillas

Shredded lettuce,
for serving

1. In a large bowl, combine the onion, garlic, soy sauce, oregano, cumin, pepper, smoked paprika, lime juice, and sliced mushrooms.

2. Toss well until the mushrooms are saturated. Let sit for 10 minutes.

3. Heat a pan over medium heat. Add the olive oil. When the oil is hot, add the mushroom mixture and cook for 5 minutes. Cover and cook for 10 more minutes, until the mushrooms and onions are soft.

4. With your fork, begin to pull apart the cap and stem of the mushrooms until they are shredded. Set the pan aside.

5. Heat a large skillet over medium heat. Heat the tortillas in the skillet for 1 to 2 minutes.

6. Stuff the tortillas with the mushroom mixture and top with lettuce and lime juice. Serve immediately.

Time-Saving Tip: You can buy minced garlic in the grocery store.

PER SERVING: Calories: 311; Total fat: 17g; Total carbs: 38g; Fiber: 7g; Sugar: 6g; Protein: 9g; Sodium: 1,388mg

Whole-Wheat Smoked Salmon Wrap

DAIRY-FREE, NUT-FREE, 30-MINUTE

Smoked salmon is delicious, healthy, and easy to use. You can find it in the seafood section of your local grocery store. The salmon gives this hearty wrap a healthy dose of omegas, as does the avocado. Baby spinach adds a refreshing element, which is especially welcome as the weather starts to get warmer. When stuffing the wrap, be careful not to overstuff, or you'll be left with a soggy wrap.

Serves 2 **Prep time: 30 minutes**

2 whole-wheat wraps or
   tortillas
2 tablespoons
   prepared hummus
1 (16-ounce) package
   smoked salmon
4 tablespoons cooked
   brown rice
½ cup baby spinach
1 tomato, sliced
1 avocado, pitted, peeled,
   and sliced
Hot sauce or salsa,
   for serving

1. Lay out the wraps. Spread 1 tablespoon of hummus on each.

2. Top the hummus evenly with the salmon.

3. Scoop 2 tablespoons of the rice onto each wrap, then layer on the spinach, tomato, and avocado, dividing them evenly.

4. Gather the stuffing on one half of the wrap. While folding in the edges of the wrap, begin to roll it tightly.

5. Serve with your favorite hot sauce or salsa.

Shopping Tip: When choosing an avocado, check under the bit of stem at the top—if it's bright green, it's ready to go. If the avocado is so soft you can make a large indent with your finger, it's too ripe.

PER SERVING: Calories: 629; Total fat: 29g; Total carbs: 42g; Fiber: 11g; Sugar: 3g; Protein: 51g; Sodium: 2,342mg

Baked Trout with Garlic and Spring Veggies

DAIRY-FREE, 5-INGREDIENT, GLUTEN-FREE, NUT-FREE, ONE POT, 30-MINUTE

A small amount of seasoning and some lemon juice are all you need to bring out the flavor of trout. High in omega-3 fatty acids, protein, and potassium, trout cooks quickly and requires minimal prep time, but it will leave you feeling satiated. The fish is paired with beautiful green roasted asparagus to add vitamins and a slightly charred flavor.

Serves 4   Prep time: 5 minutes / Cook time: 20 minutes

1 pound trout fillet

1 bunch asparagus, tough ends trimmed

3 tablespoons olive oil

½ teaspoon salt

½ teaspoon freshly ground black pepper

4 garlic cloves, peeled

1 lemon, sliced

1. Preheat the oven to 400°F. Line a baking sheet with parchment paper.

2. Place the trout and asparagus on the prepared sheet. Drizzle with the olive oil and sprinkle with the salt and pepper.

3. Place the garlic on the trout and asparagus and lay the lemon over the trout.

4. Bake for 15 to 20 minutes, until the trout is cooked through and the asparagus are tender. Remove from the oven and let cool.

5. Remove the baked lemon slices and serve. You can add a squeeze of lemon juice for extra flavor.

Shopping Tip: Buy wild-caught trout, rather than farm-raised, when possible. The flavor and nutrient profiles are better.

Prep Tip: Trim 1 to 2 inches from the bottom of the asparagus stalks; these woody ends are tougher than the rest of the stalk.

PER SERVING: Calories: 268; Total fat: 16g; Total carbs: 6g; Fiber: 3g; Sugar: 2g; Protein: 25g; Sodium: 296mg

Chicken Udon Noodles with Turnips and Peas

DAIRY-FREE, NUT-FREE

This udon noodle recipe is filled with nutritious ingredients. Peas are rich in vitamins K, C, and A and are a slightly sweet addition to this otherwise savory meal. Thicker than spaghetti, udon noodles soak up whatever delicious sauce you serve with them. Omit the chicken to make this recipe vegan.

Serves 2   **Prep time: 15 minutes / Cook time: 25 minutes**

**8 ounces dried
  udon noodles**
1 tablespoon olive oil
8 ounces ground chicken
**½ teaspoon freshly
  ground black pepper**
½ cup soy sauce
3 tablespoons rice vinegar
4 turnips, sliced
**½ (16-ounce) package
  frozen peas, or 8 ounces
  fresh peas**

1. Bring a large pot of water to a boil over high heat. Add the udon noodles and cook according to the package instructions. Drain and set aside.

2. In a large skillet, heat the oil over medium heat. Add the chicken and season with pepper. Cook, stirring, for 10 minutes, or until the chicken is cooked through.

3. Add the noodles, soy sauce, and vinegar to the skillet and stir to combine. Cook until the noodles are saturated in the sauce, 2 to 3 minutes. Remove from the heat.

4. Add the turnips and peas to the skillet and stir until the vegetables are evenly distributed. Serve immediately.

Shopping Tip: You can find udon noodles in the international food aisle of almost any grocery store, as well as at Asian markets. If you are unable to get them, use egg-based noodles instead.

PER SERVING: Calories: 809; Total fat: 18g; Total carbs: 127g; Fiber: 12g; Sugar: 16g; Protein: 42g; Sodium: 4,415mg

Vegan "Tuna" Sandwich

DAIRY-FREE, NUT-FREE, 30-MINUTE, VEGAN

Think vegan *and* tuna *sound contradictory? Well, this vegan tuna sandwich is made with protein-packed chickpeas, which have the same consistency as tuna after you give them a quick spin in the food processor. This recipe is a great lunch option, and you can make it quickly in the morning.*

Serves 2   **Prep time: 20 minutes**

1 (15-ounce) can
　chickpeas, drained
　and rinsed
2 tablespoons tahini
1 teaspoon Dijon mustard
1 teaspoon maple syrup
¼ cup chopped red onion
¼ cup chopped celery
1 teaspoon capers,
　drained and rinsed
Pinch salt
Pinch freshly ground
　black pepper
4 slices whole-grain
　bread, toasted
½ head romaine lettuce
1 tomato, sliced

1. In a food processor, combine the chickpeas, tahini, mustard, maple syrup, onion, celery, capers, salt, and pepper and pulse until the chickpeas are broken down but not mushy or pureed—the mixture should have a chunky consistency.

2. Divide the chickpea mixture between 2 slices of toast, then top with the lettuce, tomato, and a second slice of toast. Serve immediately.

Substitution Tip: Gluten-free bread is a tasty alternative to whole-grain. Instead of tahini, you can use hummus or vegan mayo.

PER SERVING: Calories: 496; Total fat: 14g; Total carbs: 73g; Fiber: 17g; Sugar: 15g; Protein: 23g; Sodium: 460mg

Kimchi Cauliflower Fried Rice

DAIRY-FREE, NUT-FREE, ONE POT, 30-MINUTE, VEGETARIAN

Cauliflower rice is a great carb cutter. You can find it in the freezer section of most grocery stores or pulse cauliflower in a food processor to make your own. Kimchi adds a tangy flavor; you can buy it online or in the refrigerated section of grocery stores.

Serves 4   **Prep time: 10 minutes / Cook time: 20 minutes**

1 tablespoon olive oil
3 garlic cloves, minced
¼ cup chopped
   yellow onion
2 carrots, diced
4 cups cauliflower rice
2 tablespoons soy sauce
Pinch salt
Pinch freshly ground
   black pepper
¼ cup frozen peas
1 large egg
3 tablespoons kimchi
Juice of 1 lemon

1. In a wok, heat the olive oil over medium-high heat.
2. Add the garlic and onion and cook, stirring frequently, for 3 minutes.
3. Add the carrots and cook, stirring, for 3 minutes.
4. Add the cauliflower rice and stir to combine. Add the soy sauce, salt, pepper, and peas, cover, and cook for 6 minutes.
5. Uncover and push the cauliflower rice away from the center of the wok. Add the egg to the empty space, then stir to incorporate the cauliflower rice. Add the kimchi and cook until the egg is set. Remove from the heat.
6. Drizzle the lemon juice over the fried cauliflower rice. Serve immediately.

Meal-Prep Tip: Make a big batch of cauliflower rice ahead of time. This rice also pairs well with any protein, such as shrimp, chicken, or steak.

PER SERVING: Calories: 114; Total fat: 5g; Total carbs: 14g; Fiber: 5g; Sugar: 5g; Protein: 5g; Sodium: 694mg

BBQ Jackfruit Pulled "Pork" Sandwich

DAIRY-FREE, NUT-FREE, ONE POT, VEGAN

This pulled jackfruit sandwich has a flavor and texture that will fool meat eaters. Jackfruit boasts a variety of vitamins such as vitamins A and C, which are great for the immune system. This recipe uses store-bought barbecue sauce, making it that much more convenient.

Serves 3   **Prep time: 10 minutes / Cook time: 30 minutes**

2 tablespoons olive oil

1 yellow onion, diced

2 (14-ounce) cans jackfruit, drained and rinsed

1 cup store-bought barbecue sauce

1 tablespoon ketchup

Pinch salt

Pinch freshly ground black pepper

3 buns, toasted

½ cup shredded purple cabbage

1. In a large pan, heat the olive oil over medium-high heat. Sauté the onion for 4 minutes, until translucent.

2. Add the jackfruit, barbecue sauce, ketchup, salt, pepper, and ½ cup water. Stir and let simmer for 15 minutes.

3. With a fork, shred the jackfruit in the pan until it has the consistency of pulled pork. Cook for 5 minutes more.

4. Serve the jackfruit mixture on the toasted buns, topped with the cabbage.

5. Store any leftover jackfruit mixture in an airtight container in the freezer for up to 1 week.

Prep Tip: You can also soak the jackfruit in water for 5 minutes before draining and rinsing.

Meal-Prep Tip: Make a double serving of the jackfruit and save half to use later for tacos or to serve with rice.

PER SERVING: Calories: 619; Total fat: 11g; Total carbs: 96g; Fiber: 7g; Sugar: 88g; Protein: 5g; Sodium: 1,872mg

Risotto with Asparagus and Snap Peas

DAIRY-FREE, GLUTEN-FREE, NUT-FREE, ONE POT, VEGAN

This creamy dish is packed with sweet and savory flavors. Risotto is made with Arborio rice, which you can find at any grocery store, and the asparagus and snap peas add a burst of sweetness. Try finishing the risotto with a little bit of lemon juice to add a zesty flavor.

Serves 4   **Prep time: 10 minutes / Cook time: 30 minutes**

2 tablespoons olive oil

1 yellow onion, chopped

2 garlic cloves, minced

1½ cups uncooked Arborio rice

5 cups vegetable broth, divided

5 asparagus stalks, woody ends trimmed, cut into 1-inch pieces

3 ounces snap peas, ends trimmed

Salt

Freshly ground black pepper

Fresh pea shoots, for garnish (optional)

1. In a large pot, combine the olive oil, onion, and garlic. Sauté over medium-high heat for 4 minutes, or until the onion becomes translucent.

2. Add the rice to the pot and sauté for 2 minutes, or until the rice is coated with the oil.

3. Slowly pour in ½ cup of broth, stirring as you pour. Cook, stirring, until the rice has absorbed the broth, then continue adding the remaining broth ½ cup at a time, waiting until the rice has absorbed each addition before adding the next and stirring continuously; this should take about 15 minutes.

4. Add the asparagus and snap peas and stir to evenly distribute the vegetables. Cook, stirring, until the rice is just tender, about 10 minutes more. Season with salt and pepper. Garnish with fresh pea shoots (if using), and serve immediately.

Shopping Tip: When you pick out your asparagus, make sure you get firm green stalks. Look for purple highlights, and make sure the tips are not soft or mushy.

PER SERVING: Calories: 365; Total fat: 8g; Total carbs: 66g; Fiber: 4g; Sugar: 5g; Protein: 7g; Sodium: 222mg

Portabella Mushrooms with Spinach and Ancient Grains

DAIRY-FREE, NUT-FREE, VEGAN

Portabellas are versatile when it comes to cooking. They make an edible bowl for this hearty dish packed with B vitamins, protein, and iron. Quinoa, which is a complete protein, adds all nine essential amino acids.

Serves 4   **Prep time: 15 minutes / Cook time: 40 minutes**

1 cup uncooked
 quinoa, rinsed
4 portabella
 mushroom caps
2 teaspoons olive oil, plus
 more for brushing
Salt
Freshly ground
 black pepper
1 small onion, diced
2 garlic cloves, minced
1 cup bread crumbs
2 cups spinach
1 tablespoon
 dried oregano

1. Preheat the oven to 375°F.

2. Bring 2 cups water to a boil in a medium saucepan. Add the quinoa, reduce the heat to low, cover, and simmer for 15 minutes, or until tender.

3. While the quinoa cooks, use a spoon to remove the gills from the portabella caps.

4. Brush the caps with olive oil and season with salt and pepper.

5. In a large skillet, combine the olive oil, onion, and garlic. Cook over medium-high heat for 4 minutes, or until the onion is translucent.

6. Add the quinoa and bread crumbs to the skillet and cook, stirring, for 5 minutes. Remove from the heat.

7. Add the spinach and stir until the spinach has wilted. Add the oregano and a pinch each of salt and pepper.

8. Spoon the quinoa mixture into the mushroom caps, filling them completely.

9. Place the stuffed mushrooms on a baking sheet. Bake for 20 minutes, or until they are slightly browned. Serve immediately.

Meal-Prep Tip: Double the quinoa so you can freeze and store half for later use.

PER SERVING: Calories: 322; Total fat: 7g; Total carbs: 55g; Fiber: 7g; Sugar: 4g; Protein: 13g; Sodium: 257mg

Fish Tacos with Purple Cabbage

Tilapia is easy to find, has a mild flavor, and is delicious in tacos. It's also a good source of protein. With healthy fat from avocado and vitamins from the cabbage, this meal is rich in nutrients.

Serves 4   Prep time: 20 minutes / Cook time: 10 minutes

8 ounces tilapia fillet

1 lemon, halved

1 teaspoon ground cumin, divided

1 teaspoon paprika, divided

Salt

Freshly ground black pepper

2 tablespoons olive oil, plus more as needed

5 corn tortillas

2 tomatoes, chopped

½ head purple cabbage, chopped

2 avocados, pitted, peeled, and sliced

1. Rinse the tilapia under cold water. Place it in a baking dish and let dry.

2. When the tilapia is dry, squeeze the juice from one lemon half over it. Season with ½ teaspoon of cumin, ½ teaspoon of paprika, salt, and pepper. Refrigerate and marinate for 10 minutes.

3. In a large skillet, heat the olive oil over medium-high heat. Place the tilapia in the skillet, seasoned-side down, and cook for 3 minutes. Season the top of the fish with the remaining ½ teaspoon of cumin and ½ teaspoon of paprika, salt, and pepper, then flip the fish and cook for 3 minutes on the second side, until the fish is opaque and flakes easily with a fork. Remove from the heat.

4. Lightly coat a separate skillet with olive oil and heat it over medium heat. Add the corn tortillas and heat for 2 minutes.

5. Divide the tilapia among the tortillas and top with the tomatoes, cabbage, and avocado. Squeeze the juice from the remaining lemon half over the top and serve.

Prep Tip: Add more seasoning if it tastes too mild.

Substitution Tip: If you don't like fish, this recipe also works with steak, chicken, or even tofu!

PER SERVING: Calories: 356; Total fat: 22g; Total carbs: 29g; Fiber: 11g; Sugar: 5g; Protein: 16g; Sodium: 102mg

Portabella "Steak" with Fresh Herbs

DAIRY-FREE, 5-INGREDIENT, NUT-FREE, 30-MINUTE, VEGAN

Portabella mushrooms are very absorbent, so tread lightly with the balsamic vinegar in this recipe. This portabella steak pairs amazingly well with potatoes and is reminiscent of a real steak dinner—even meat eaters will be going for seconds. Instead of baking the mushrooms, you can grill them to add an even more realistic steak flavor or simply cook them in a pan on the stovetop.

Serves 2 **Prep time: 5 minutes / Cook time: 20 minutes**

**2 portabella
  mushroom caps**
2 tablespoons olive oil
**2 tablespoons
  balsamic vinegar**
**2 tablespoons steak
  seasoning**
**Fresh rosemary,
  coarsely chopped**
Fresh bread, for serving

1. Preheat the oven to 400°F.
2. Place the mushroom caps gills up in a shallow baking dish. Drizzle with the olive oil and vinegar and sprinkle with the steak seasoning and rosemary.
3. Bake for 10 minutes. Flip the caps over and bake for another 10 minutes.
4. Remove from the oven and serve with bread.

Prep Tip: Coarsely chopping the rosemary releases its aroma, increasing the herb flavor in the dish.

PER SERVING: Calories: 146; Total fat: 14g; Total carbs: 5g; Fiber: 1g; Sugar: 2g; Protein: 2g; Sodium: 6mg

Spring Vegan Quiche

DAIRY-FREE, GLUTEN-FREE, VEGAN

Quiche makes a perfect weekend brunch—or any other meal, for that matter. Nutritional yeast gives this vegan version its cheesy flavor. This quiche is easily customizable, so add any vegetables you have on hand.

Serves 2   **Prep time: 15 minutes / Cook time: 40 minutes**

1 (14-ounce) block
   firm tofu
3 tablespoons
   nondairy milk
3 tablespoons
   nutritional yeast
1 tablespoon ground
   turmeric
Pinch salt
Pinch freshly ground
   black pepper
2 tablespoons olive oil
3 garlic cloves, minced
1 yellow onion, chopped
1 cup chopped
   mushrooms
3 collard green
   leaves, chopped
1 cup spinach
½ cup broccoli florets
1 tablespoon black salt
   (optional)

1. Preheat the oven to 375°F.

2. In a food processor, combine the tofu, milk, nutritional yeast, turmeric, salt, and pepper. Process for about 1 minute and set aside.

3. In a cast-iron skillet, heat the olive oil over medium heat. Add the garlic and onion and sauté for 4 minutes. Add the mushrooms and sauté for another 4 minutes.

4. Add the collard greens, spinach, and broccoli. Remove from the heat. Stir until the leaves begin to wilt.

5. Pour the tofu mixture into the skillet over the vegetables. Season with the black salt (if using).

6. Place the skillet in the oven and bake for 30 minutes. Remove from the oven and let cool.

7. Cut the quiche into wedges and serve immediately.

Substitution Tip: Use eggs instead of tofu if you want a more traditional quiche or for anyone with a soy allergy.

PER SERVING: Calories: 401; Total fat: 23g; Total carbs: 28g; Fiber: 13g; Sugar: 4g; Protein: 30g; Sodium: 3,023mg

Sweet Potato Crust Pizza

DAIRY-FREE, 5-INGREDIENT, NUT-FREE, VEGAN

This pizza crust is delicious, nutrient dense, and convenient to make for lunch or dinner. The sweet potato gives the crust its starchy foundation and slight sweetness. Keep in mind that the baking time depends on the thickness of the crust. The thicker the crust, the longer it will need in the oven, so make it thinner if you are tight on time.

Serves 4   **Prep time: 10 minutes / Cook time: 50 minutes**

2 sweet potatoes, peeled and chopped
1 cup all-purpose flour
¼ cup cornstarch
2 tablespoons flaxseed meal
½ teaspoon salt

1. Preheat the oven to 425°F. Line a baking sheet with parchment paper.

2. In a medium saucepan, bring 2 cups water to a boil over high heat. Add the sweet potatoes to the boiling water and cook for 15 minutes or until they are soft. Drain and let cool, then transfer to a bowl and mash.

3. Transfer 2 cups of the mashed sweet potato to a large bowl (save any extra for another use). Add the flour, cornstarch, flaxseed meal, and salt. Mix well.

4. Transfer the dough to the center of the prepared sheet.

5. Using another piece of parchment paper, press down on the dough gently with your hands to flatten it into an even circle. Peel off the top sheet of parchment and bake for 20 minutes.

6. Remove from the oven and add your toppings as desired, then bake for 10 minutes more.

7. Remove from the oven and let cool for 5 minutes. Slice and serve immediately.

Prep Tip: Make the crust as even as possible so it will cook uniformly. If you end up with too much dough, you can make multiple smaller pizza crusts. The crust freezes well—just wrap it in aluminum foil or place in a zip-top bag and store in the freezer for up to 1 month.

PER SERVING: Calories: 219; Total fat: 1g; Total carbs: 45g; Fiber: 4g; Sugar: 3g; Protein: 5g; Sodium: 329mg

Crusted Cabbage Steaks

DAIRY-FREE, 5-INGREDIENT, GLUTEN-FREE, NUT-FREE, VEGAN

This recipe has roots in Eastern Europe, where cabbage and potatoes are staples. Cabbage boasts tons of vitamins and minerals such as vitamins K and C, folate, and manganese, and it is great for digestion because of its high amount of insoluble fiber, which feeds the healthy bacteria in our gut. Pair this dish with any protein you'd like, or use it as a filling for a sandwich.

Serves 4   **Prep time: 10 minutes / Cook time: 30 minutes**

2 heads green cabbage, cut into 1-inch-thick slices

3 tablespoons olive oil, divided

1 teaspoon garlic powder, divided

1 teaspoon salt, divided

1. Preheat the oven to 400°F. Line a baking sheet with parchment paper.
2. Place the cabbage "steaks" on the prepared sheet, spacing them ½ inch apart.
3. Brush half the olive oil over the cabbage, then season with half the garlic powder and half the salt. Flip the steaks and repeat with the remaining oil, garlic powder, and salt.
4. Bake the steaks for 30 minutes, or until crispy, flipping them once halfway through the cooking time.
5. Serve warm. Wrap leftovers tightly in plastic wrap and store in the refrigerator for up to 2 days to add to salads or casseroles.

Shopping Tip: When you pick out a cabbage, make sure the color is vibrant and bright. As soon as you cut your cabbage, it begins to lose vitamin C, so cook it right away.

PER SERVING: Calories: 182; Total fat: 11g; Total carbs: 21g; Fiber: 9g; Sugar: 12g; Protein: 5g; Sodium: 646mg

One-Bite Dumplings

DAIRY-FREE, NUT-FREE, VEGAN

This Asian-inspired recipe uses premade wonton wrappers, which you can purchase in the refrigerated vegan section at grocery stores or at Asian markets. These dumplings are versatile—you can stuff them with most vegetables and proteins, or try panfrying them to make them crunchy. Serve them with soy sauce for dipping. You can also make extra, freeze them until solid on a baking sheet, then store them frozen for up to a month. When you're ready to eat them, dump them into boiling water and cook for 10 minutes.

Serves 2   **Prep time: 20 minutes / Cook time: 20 minutes**

2 tablespoons olive oil
2 garlic cloves, minced
1 onion, finely chopped
1 ounce mushrooms, finely chopped
½ head green cabbage, finely chopped
1 carrot, thinly shredded
Pinch salt
Pinch freshly ground black pepper
1 (8-ounce) package wonton wrappers
Soy sauce, for serving

1. Bring a large pot of water to a boil.

2. In a large pan, heat the olive oil over medium-high heat. Add the garlic and onion and cook for 4 minutes. Add the mushrooms, cabbage, carrot, salt, and pepper and cook for 5 minutes. Remove from the heat and let cool slightly.

3. Lay the wonton wrappers flat on your work surface. Scoop a small portion of the mushroom mixture into the center of a wrapper, fold the wrapper in half to form a triangle and enclose the filling, and press down the along the edges to seal. Repeat with the remaining wrappers and filling.

4. Working in batches, if necessary, add the wontons to the boiling water and cook for 5 minutes, then scoop them out with a slotted spoon and transfer to a large plate. Repeat with the remaining dumplings.

5. Let cool slightly, then serve with soy sauce.

PER SERVING: Calories: 538; Total fat: 16g; Total carbs: 86g; Fiber: 9g; Sugar: 10g; Protein: 15g; Sodium: 932mg

Lemon Asparagus Pasta

DAIRY-FREE, ONE POT, 30-MINUTE, VEGAN

The coconut milk gives this pasta a sweet creaminess. The lemon adds an extra boost of vitamin C. The asparagus packs in healthy vitamins and minerals such as vitamins A, E, K, and B$_6$, folate, iron, copper, and calcium. When you're shopping for asparagus, look for bright green stalks and firm stems.

Serves 2   **Prep time: 5 minutes / Cook time: 25 minutes**

2 tablespoons olive oil
1 pound asparagus,
    bottom inch trimmed
1 small onion, chopped
2 cups vegetable broth
1 (9-ounce) box pasta
½ cup canned
    coconut milk
Juice of 1 lemon, plus
    more for serving
Salt
Freshly ground
    black pepper

1. In a large pot, heat the olive oil over medium heat. Sauté the asparagus for 5 minutes, until tender. Remove the asparagus and set aside.

2. In the same pot, sauté the onion for 3 to 4 minutes.

3. Add the broth and bring to a boil. Add the pasta and cook for 15 minutes, or until al dente. Slowly stir in the coconut milk, then add the asparagus and lemon juice. Season with salt and pepper.

4. Cook for 2 more minutes, until the noodles absorb the sauce.

5. Serve with a squeeze of lemon juice over the top.

Substitution Tip: Protein such as chicken or shrimp pairs great with this dish.

PER SERVING: Calories: 943; Total fat: 28g; Total carbs: 152g; Fiber: 12g; Sugar: 50g; Protein: 23g; Sodium: 648mg

Honey-Glazed Tofu Chops with Seasonal Greens

DAIRY-FREE, 5-INGREDIENT, NUT-FREE, ONE POT, VEGETARIAN

Tofu has endless cooking possibilities because of its mild flavor, and it also contains beneficial nutrients like protein and iron. The key to good tofu is the sauce and the amount of time in the pan: the longer tofu cooks, the crispier—and more delicious— it gets.

Serves 2   **Prep time: 5 minutes / Cook time: 30 minutes**

2 tablespoons olive oil

1 (14-ounce) block
   extra-firm tofu, cubed

1 tablespoon soy sauce

2 tablespoons honey

5 collard green
   leaves, chopped

8 ounces spinach

1. In a nonstick pan, heat the olive oil over medium-high heat. Once the oil is hot, add the tofu.

2. Add the soy sauce and honey and cook the tofu for 15 minutes.

3. Flip the tofu and cook for 10 minutes more.

4. Add the collard greens, spinach, and 1 tablespoon water. Cover and cook until the greens are wilted and tender.

5. Serve immediately.

Prep Tip: When you remove the tofu from the package, wrap it in a paper towel and gently press out the excess water.

PER SERVING: Calories: 502; Total fat: 31g; Total carbs: 32g; Fiber: 8g; Sugar: 19g; Protein: 30g; Sodium: 573mg

Jap Chae Vegetable Medley

This noodle dish is a great way to incorporate leftover produce. You can find sweet potato noodles in most grocery stores, but pad thai noodles will work. Typically, this dish is served cold, but it tastes amazing warm. Garnish it with cilantro, peanuts, and fresh lime juice to make it even more delicious.

Serves 4   **Prep time: 10 minutes / Cook time: 15 minutes**

2 (3.5-ounce) packages sweet potato noodles
2 tablespoons olive oil
2 garlic cloves, minced
1 carrot, cut into matchsticks
6 ounces mushrooms, chopped or sliced
6 ounces broccoli florets
½ head green cabbage, chopped or sliced
3 tablespoons soy sauce
1 large egg
1 tablespoon sesame seeds, for garnish (optional)
Chopped scallions, for garnish (optional)

1. Bring a medium pot of water to a boil. Add the sweet potato noodles and cook according to the package instructions. Drain and set aside.

2. In a wok, heat the olive oil over low heat. Add the garlic and cook for 3 minutes. Add the carrot, mushrooms, broccoli, cabbage, and soy sauce. Cook, stirring continuously, for 5 minutes.

3. Add the egg and stir to combine. Cook, stirring, until the egg is set, 4 minutes.

4. Add the sweet potato noodles and stir to combine with the sauce and vegetables. Toss and cook until the noodles have soaked up the sauce.

5. Serve immediately, garnished with sesame seeds and scallions (if using).

Time-Saving Tip: Buy your broccoli florets pre-packaged in the fresh or frozen section.

PER SERVING: Calories: 528; Total fat: 9g; Total carbs: 104g; Fiber: 8g; Sugar: 5g; Protein: 12g; Sodium: 735mg

SUMMERTIME GAZPACHO
PAGE 46

chapter three summer

June Through August

Summer is the season for peppers, carrots, corn, eggplant, green peas, and squash.

Summertime Gazpacho

This quintessential summer soup from Spain highlights sweet summer flavors. This version makes the prep easy. Serve the soup garnished with halved cherry tomatoes and freshly ground black pepper.

Serves 2   **Prep time: 10 minutes / Cook time: 10 minutes**

2 pints cherry tomatoes, plus more for serving

1 red bell pepper, chopped

1 English cucumber, peeled and chopped

1/2 red onion, chopped

2 garlic cloves, minced

1/4 cup olive oil

1 tablespoon red wine vinegar

Juice of 1 lemon

Pinch salt

Pinch freshly ground black pepper

1 teaspoon Worcestershire sauce

1/2 cup vegetable broth or chicken broth, plus more as needed

1. In a blender, combine the tomatoes, red bell pepper, cucumber, onion, garlic, olive oil, vinegar, lemon juice, salt, pepper, Worcestershire sauce, and vegetable broth, and blend until smooth. If the soup is too thick, add some additional broth to thin it as desired.

2. Serve immediately or refrigerate until ready to serve. You can store the soup in an airtight container in the freezer for up to 2 days.

Meal-Prep Tip: Prep extra vegetables when making this dish so you have them on hand to toss in a salad or an omelet for an other meal.

PER SERVING: Calories: 358; Total fat: 27g; Total carbs: 31g; Fiber: 7g; Sugar: 17g; Protein: 7g; Sodium: 263mg

Spicy Pho with Edamame

DAIRY-FREE, GLUTEN-FREE, NUT-FREE, VEGAN

Soup often evokes thoughts of winter. Not pho. It originated in Vietnam, where the weather is typically hot. (Although counterintuitive, eating spicy foods in the summer can have a cooling effect on the body.) This recipe uses store-bought pho broth, which can be found in many grocery stores, but vegetable or chicken broth will work fine.

Serves 2   **Prep time: 10 minutes / Cook time: 30 minutes**

5 cups vegan pho broth
1 (3-inch) piece fresh
   ginger, peeled and sliced
4 ounces mushrooms
2 carrots, cut into thin
   matchsticks
1 jalapeño, sliced
4 ounces rice noodles
½ cup frozen edamame
Mung bean sprouts,
   for garnish
Fresh mint or cilantro,
   for garnish
1 lime, quartered
   lengthwise

1. In a medium pot, heat the broth over low heat.
2. Add the ginger, cover, and cook for 15 minutes.
3. Add the mushrooms and the carrots and cook for 5 minutes.
4. Add 3 slices of the jalapeño to the broth. Put the rice noodles in the pot, cover, and cook for 4 minutes, or until the noodles are soft.
5. Add the edamame and cook for 1 minute, then turn off the heat.
6. Ladle the soup into a large bowl and garnish with the remaining jalapeño slices (if you like heat), mung bean sprouts, and fresh herbs. Serve immediately, with lime wedges for squeezing over the top.

Cooking Tip: Omit the jalapeño if you prefer less heat.

PER SERVING: Calories: 411; Total fat: 2g; Total carbs: 80g; Fiber: 6g; Sugar: 18g; Protein: 19g; Sodium: 1,808mg

Corn and Sweet Pepper Tamales

DAIRY-FREE, GLUTEN-FREE, NUT-FREE, VEGAN

Tamales, a Mexican staple, require two essential items: dried corn husks and masa harina, a special type of corn flour. You can order both online or find them in the international food aisle of your grocery store. Pair the tamales with your favorite hot sauce for a perfect summer meal.

Serves 4   **Prep time: 20 minutes / Cook time: 45 minutes**

1 (15-ounce) package dried corn husks

3 cups masa harina

1 teaspoon baking powder

2 cups vegetable broth

1 tablespoon olive oil

1 yellow onion, chopped

1 yellow bell pepper, diced

1 red bell pepper, diced

1 teaspoon Mexican seasoning

1 (15-ounce) can corn, drained

1. Soak the corn husks in a bowl of hot water.

2. In a large bowl, whisk together the masa harina and baking powder. Pour in the broth and mix until a dough forms. Set aside.

3. In a large skillet, heat the olive oil over medium heat. Add the onion and cook for 4 minutes, or until translucent.

4. Add the bell peppers and Mexican seasoning and cook for 3 minutes, stirring frequently.

5. Add the corn and mix until it is distributed evenly. Cook for 2 minutes, turn off the heat, and set aside.

6. Fill a large pot with 3 inches of water. Place a steamer basket in the pot. Bring the water to a boil over high heat.

7. Lay a corn husk flat on your work surface. Scoop about ⅓ cup of the masa dough into the middle of the corn husk and spread it evenly. Place 1 tablespoon of the vegetable mixture in the center of the masa dough.

8. Fold the corn husk in half, so the outside edges of the dough seal together and enclose the filling, then wrap the tamale firmly in the corn husk. Seal the tamale with the right side of the corn husk and then the left side of the husk. Fold the top of the corn husk down onto the tamale. Repeat with the remaining masa dough and filling.

9. Place the tamales in the steamer, cover, and steam for 30 minutes. (Keep an eye on the water in the pot and add more if needed.)

10. Using tongs, remove the tamales from the steamer and place them on a serving dish. Let cool. Serve immediately.

Meal-Prep Tip: Tamales freeze very well. Make extra to freeze in an airtight container for up to 1 month.

PER SERVING: Calories: 419; Total fat: 7g; Total carbs: 83g; Fiber: 11g; Sugar: 6g; Protein: 10g; Sodium: 318mg

Falafel Pita with Cucumber, Tomato, and Tahini

DAIRY-FREE, NUT-FREE, ONE POT, 30-MINUTE, VEGAN

Falafel is a favorite of vegans and vegetarians because of its flavor and high protein content. Make sure to let the chickpeas dry before making the falafel. To speed up the process, spread them over a baking sheet and pop them in the oven on the lowest temperature for 5 to 10 minutes.

Serves 2   **Prep time: 10 minutes / Cook time: 15 minutes**

½ cup fresh
   parsley, chopped
1 small onion
2 garlic cloves, minced
1 teaspoon ground cumin
1 teaspoon ground
   coriander
1 teaspoon
   all-purpose flour
Juice of ½ lemon
1 (15-ounce) can
   chickpeas, drained
   and rinsed
3 tablespoons olive oil
Tahini, for serving
2 pita breads
1 tomato, sliced
1 cucumber, peeled,
   seeded, and sliced

1. In a food processor, combine the parsley, onion, garlic, cumin, coriander, and flour. Process until coarse.

2. Add the lemon juice and chickpeas and pulse 7 times just to coarsely chop the chickpeas. Transfer the mixture to a large bowl.

3. In a large nonstick pan, heat the olive oil over medium heat.

4. Roll the chickpea mixture into golf ball–size balls and lightly flatten them. Working in batches, if necessary, add the falafel to the hot oil and cook for 7 minutes, or until they are golden, then flip and cook for 7 minutes on the other side.

5. Spread a layer of tahini inside each pita, then add a layer of tomato, cucumber, and falafel. Serve immediately.

6. You can store leftover falafel in an airtight container in the refrigerator for up to 1 day. They are also delicious with rice and hummus.

Prep Tip: When cooking don't overcrowd the pan—leave some space between the falafel.

PER SERVING: Calories: 574; Total fat: 29g; Total carbs: 67g; Fiber: 14g; Sugar: 12g; Protein: 18g; Sodium: 195mg

Smoked Salmon Frittata Muffins

DAIRY-FREE, GLUTEN-FREE

This frittata is rich in omega-3 fatty acids, B vitamins, and protein. This recipe uses a muffin tin to make delicious individual-size frittatas, but you can combine the ingredients in a pie pan or a cast-iron skillet to make one large frittata instead. Place the vegetables in the pan, pour the egg mixture over them, and bake as directed.

Serves 2   **Prep time: 10 minutes / Cook time: 15 minutes**

Olive oil, for greasing

5 eggs

½ cup unsweetened nondairy milk

2 tablespoons chopped fresh dill

2 garlic cloves, minced

8 cherry tomatoes, sliced

7 ounces smoked salmon

1. Preheat the oven to 350°F. Grease a standard 12-cup muffin tin with olive oil.

2. In a large bowl, whisk together the eggs, milk, dill, and garlic until thoroughly combined.

3. Divide the cherry tomatoes and smoked salmon evenly among the wells of the prepared tin. Pour the egg mixture over the tomatoes and salmon, filling each well three-quarters full.

4. Bake for 15 minutes, or until the eggs are cooked through. Remove from the oven and let cool in the muffin tin for 5 minutes.

5. Remove the individual quiches and serve immediately.

Prep Tip: Make sure you leave room at the top of the wells of the muffin tin when pouring in the egg mixture; the frittatas will expand in the oven.

PER SERVING: Calories: 423; Total fat: 19g; Total carbs: 27g; Fiber: 7g; Sugar: 16g; Protein: 40g; Sodium: 260mg

Lemon Salmon with Green Beans

DAIRY-FREE, 5-INGREDIENT, GLUTEN-FREE, NUT-FREE, ONE POT, 30-MINUTE

Lemon and salmon make a great flavor combination, especially when paired with green beans and garlic. This dish is light, refreshing, and certain to leave you satisfied. You can replace the fresh green beans with frozen ones to save some prep time. A cast-iron skillet will help the salmon cook evenly.

Serves 2   **Prep time: 5 minutes / Cook time: 20 minutes**

**2 pounds skin-on
   salmon fillets**
2 tablespoons olive oil
1 pound green beans
3 garlic cloves, minced
Salt
**Freshly ground
   black pepper**
1 lemon, sliced

1. Preheat the oven to 400°F.

2. Rinse the salmon under cold water for 5 minutes and pat dry with a paper towel.

3. In a cast-iron skillet, combine the olive oil, green beans, garlic, and a pinch each of salt and pepper. Toss to coat the green beans in the olive oil.

4. Move the green beans to the side of the pan. Add the salmon to the skillet skin-side down. Season the salmon with salt and pepper and lay 4 lemon slices on top.

5. Cover the skillet with aluminum foil or an oven-safe lid, place in the oven, and bake for 20 minutes, until the salmon is opaque and light pink and flakes easily with a fork. Serve immediately.

Shopping Tip: Look for firm, light green beans.

PER SERVING: Calories: 507; Total fat: 36g; Total carbs: 20g; Fiber: 9g; Sugar: 3g; Protein: 30g; Sodium: 162mg

Savory Chickpea Crepe with Summer Harvest

DAIRY-FREE, GLUTEN-FREE, NUT-FREE, 30-MINUTE, VEGAN

Chickpea crepes pair beautifully with summer vegetables, and chickpea flour is high in protein and makes for a batter thinner than that of typical pancake batter. Remember that the more batter you add to the pan, the longer it will take to cook.

Serves 4 **Prep time: 10 minutes / Cook time: 10 minutes**

---

2 cups chickpea flour
½ teaspoon salt
½ teaspoon garlic powder
1 tablespoon olive oil
1 avocado, pitted, peeled, and sliced
1 bell pepper, sliced
1 tomato, sliced
Hummus, for serving (optional)
Lemon wedges, for serving (optional)
Leafy greens, for serving (optional)

1. In a blender, combine the chickpea flour, 1½ cups water, salt, and garlic powder and blend on high speed until smooth. Let the batter stand for a minute to allow some of the bubbles to subside.

2. In a large nonstick skillet, heat the olive oil over medium-low heat.

3. Slowly pour about ¼ cup of the batter into the skillet. Cook for about 3 minutes, until the edges start to bubble. Flip and cook for another 3 minutes, or until firm. Transfer the crepe to a plate and repeat to cook the remaining batter.

4. Divide the avocado, bell pepper, and tomato among the crepes, placing them in the center.

5. Fold each crepe in half to form a half-moon, matching up the edges as evenly as possible and pressing down on the edges, then fold in half again to form a triangle.

6. Top with hummus or a squeeze of lemon (if using). Serve immediately with a side of leafy greens (if using).

Shopping Tip: This recipe works for most vegetables. Buy seasonal produce.

PER SERVING: Calories: 324; Total fat: 17g; Total carbs: 34g; Fiber: 9g; Sugar: 7g; Protein: 12g; Sodium: 325mg

Cucumber and Shrimp with Rice

DAIRY-FREE, NUT-FREE, 30-MINUTE

This Southeast Asian–inspired dish is quick, refreshing, and very nutritious. Cucumbers provide tons of vitamins and minerals. Shrimp is packed with protein.

Serves 2   **Prep time: 10 minutes / Cook time: 20 minutes**

2 tablespoons olive oil

1 pound shrimp, peeled and deveined

1 (½-inch) piece fresh ginger, peeled and sliced

2 tablespoons soy sauce

1 teaspoon hoisin sauce

1 teaspoon sriracha

Juice of 2 limes

1 teaspoon brown sugar

1 large cucumber, halved and thinly sliced

2 cups cooked jasmine rice

½ cup chopped fresh basil

½ cup chopped fresh mint

1. In a large skillet, heat the olive oil over medium-high heat. Add the shrimp and cook for 1 minute on each side. Remove the shrimp from the skillet and place on a plate.

2. In the same skillet, cook the ginger for 2 minutes.

3. Add the soy sauce, hoisin sauce, sriracha, lime juice, and brown sugar and cook, stirring frequently, for 2 minutes.

4. Return the shrimp to the skillet, stirring to coat in the sauce. Cook for 7 minutes.

5. Add the cucumber and stir. Turn off the heat.

6. Spoon a bed of rice onto each serving plate. Top with the shrimp and sauce. Garnish with the basil and mint. Serve immediately.

Time-Saving Tip: You can buy frozen shrimp to save prep time.

PER SERVING: Calories: 564; Total fat: 10g; Total carbs: 63g; Fiber: 3g; Sugar: 3g; Protein: 54g; Sodium: 1,412mg

Polenta Cakes with Red Sauce

GLUTEN-FREE, 5-INGREDIENT, NUT-FREE, VEGETARIAN

Polenta is a great substitute for pasta. This Italian staple is made of ground yellow corn cooked with water or broth. For convenience, this dish calls for prepackaged polenta and store-bought pasta sauce.

Serves 2   **Prep time: 10 minutes / Cook time: 25 minutes**

2 (16- to 18-ounce) rolls
 prepared polenta
2 tablespoons olive
 oil, divided
½ onion, chopped
1 tomato, diced
1 (25-ounce) jar
 marinara sauce
Grated Parmesan cheese,
 for serving

1. Upwrap the polenta rolls and cut them crosswise into ½-inch-thick rounds.

2. In a large nonstick skillet, heat 1 tablespoon of olive oil over medium heat. Working in batches as needed, add the polenta cakes and cook for 5 minutes, or until golden brown on the bottom. Flip and cook until golden brown on the other side, about 5 minutes more. Transfer the polenta cakes to a plate, cover to keep warm, and set aside.

3. Meanwhile, in a separate large skillet, heat the remaining 1 tablespoon of olive oil over medium heat. Add the onion and cook for 4 minutes.

4. Add the tomato and cook for 4 minutes, stirring frequently.

5. Pour in the marinara sauce, reduce the heat to low, and stir. Cook for 6 minutes, then turn off the heat.

6. Lay the polenta cakes on a serving plate and pour the sauce over them. Sprinkle with Parmesan and serve immediately.

Shopping Tip: You can find rolls of prepared polenta in the pasta section at the grocery store.

PER SERVING: Calories: 572; Total fat: 15g; Total carbs: 92g; Fiber: 12g; Sugar: 23g; Protein: 14g; Sodium: 1,900mg

Southern Black Bean Burger

If you typically have a beef burger at a summer barbecue but are trying to eat more vegetables (and less store-bought processed food, such as veggie patties), try this black bean burger. Quick to make, it's also packed with nutrient-dense whole foods and protein. Be sure you make enough to share.

Serves 4   **Prep time: 15 minutes / Cook time: 25 minutes**

2 (15-ounce) cans
   black beans, drained
   and rinsed
2 eggs
2 cups shredded carrot
1 cup bread crumbs
½ teaspoon salt
½ teaspoon
   baking powder
½ teaspoon chili powder
1 teaspoon smoked
   paprika
1 tablespoon olive oil
4 hamburger buns
Toppings of your choice

1. In a large bowl, combine the black beans, eggs, carrot, bread crumbs, salt, baking powder, chili powder, and paprika. Using a fork, mash until well combined.

2. Shape about ½ cup of the bean mixture into a patty about ¾ inch thick. Set the patty on a large plate and repeat with the remaining bean mixture.

3. In a large skillet, heat the olive oil over medium heat. Place the patties in the skillet (work in batches, if necessary) and cook for about 5 minutes on each side, until crispy and heated through.

4. Serve the patties on the buns, topped with your favorite burger fixings.

Meal-Prep Tip: These burgers freeze very well. Wrap each tightly in aluminum foil or plastic wrap and freeze up to 1 month. If you need lunch or dinner in a pinch, just grab them from the freezer, defrost, and cook as directed.

PER SERVING: Calories: 364; Total fat: 8g; Total carbs: 56g; Fiber: 14g; Sugar: 5g; Protein: 18g; Sodium: 562mg

Stuffed Bell Peppers with Lentils and Brown Rice

GLUTEN-FREE, NUT-FREE, VEGETARIAN

Sweet-tasting bell peppers make the perfect bowl for this recipe's nutrient-dense lentil stuffing, which is also tasty in tacos or lettuce wraps. Red bell peppers are the sweetest. Yellow bell peppers have the most vitamin C.

Serves 4   **Prep time: 15 minutes / Cook time: 30 minutes**

**4 large bell peppers,
   halved and seeded
2 tablespoons olive oil
2 garlic cloves, minced
½ yellow onion, chopped
2 small zucchini, chopped
2 cups cooked brown rice
1 cup cooked lentils
Salt
Freshly ground
   black pepper
1 cup shredded mozzarella
   cheese (optional)
Chopped fresh
   herbs, such
   as parsley, for serving**

1. Preheat the oven to 425°F.

2. Arrange the bell pepper halves in a roasting pan cut-side up so they sit like cups.

3. In a large skillet, heat the olive oil over medium-low heat. Add the garlic and onion and cook for 3 minutes, or until the onion is translucent. Add the zucchini and cook, stirring, for 3 minutes.

4. Add the rice and lentils to the skillet, season with salt and pepper, and stir. Remove from the heat.

5. Using a spoon, fill the bell pepper halves with the rice mixture, stuffing each to the brim.

6. Bake the stuffed peppers for 15 minutes. Top each with the mozzarella (if using), dividing it evenly, then bake for 5 minutes more, until the cheese has melted.

7. Remove the peppers from the oven and garnish with chopped herbs.

8. If you have extra stuffing, store it in an airtight container in the refrigerator for up to 2 days.

Substitution Tip: You can add protein such as ground beef.

PER SERVING: Calories: 277; Total fat: 8g; Total carbs: 45g; Fiber: 9g; Sugar: 14g; Protein: 10g; Sodium: 691mg

Quinoa Burrito Bowl

DAIRY-FREE, GLUTEN-FREE, NUT-FREE, 30-MINUTE, VEGAN

This burrito bowl—all the great fillings you love in a burrito, minus the tortilla—is perfect for a quick meal. The corn adds sweetness. The quinoa adds all the essential amino acids. You can serve this dish as the filling for a taco or you can wrap it in a tortilla for a traditional burrito.

Serves 2   **Prep time: 15 minutes / Cook time: 15 minutes**

2 cups quinoa, rinsed

1 small onion, chopped

1 tablespoon olive oil

2 tomatoes, chopped

2 (15-ounce) cans black beans

1 bell pepper, sliced

Salt

Freshly ground black pepper

½ cup fresh or frozen corn

1 avocado, pitted, peeled, and sliced

1. In a medium pot, bring 3½ cups water to a boil. Add the quinoa, bring back to a boil, and reduce the heat to maintain a simmer. Cover and cook for 15 minutes, or until the white outer ring of the quinoa begins to detach itself.

2. In a large skillet, cook the onion in the oil over medium heat. Add the tomatoes and cook for 3 minutes. Add the beans and bell pepper. Season with salt and pepper. Cook on low heat for 6 minutes.

3. Place a layer of quinoa in 2 bowls. Top with the bean mixture, corn, and avocado.

4. Store the bean mixture in an airtight container in the refrigerator for up to 2 days.

Substitution Tip: You can replace the black beans with pinto beans, if you prefer.

PER SERVING: Calories: 800; Total fat: 19g; Total carbs: 127g; Fiber: 36g; Sugar: 9g; Protein: 36g; Sodium: 39mg

Fresh Green Sandwich

NUT-FREE, 30-MINUTE, VEGETARIAN

This sandwich is essentially a healthy green salad between two slices of whole-grain bread. The cucumber and yogurt add a nice cooling effect, which is necessary during hot summer months.

Serves 2   **Prep time: 10 minutes**

¼ **cup chopped fresh dill**
¼ **cup plain Greek yogurt**
Juice of 1 lemon
**3 tablespoons olive oil,
  plus more for drizzling**
Salt
Freshly ground pepper
**1 cucumber, seeded,
  peeled, and cut into
  thin strips**
4 slices whole-grain bread
**4 ounces fresh
  basil leaves**
4 ounces sprouts

1. In a bowl, mix the dill, yogurt, and half the lemon juice until combined. Slowly add the olive oil, then season with salt and pepper, and mix until blended with a fork or whisk. Set aside.

2. Place the cucumber in a separate bowl, drizzle with olive oil and the remaining lemon juice, and season with salt and pepper.

3. Spread a light layer of the yogurt mixture over the top of each slice of bread.

4. Top two slices of bread with a layer of cucumber, basil leaves, and sprouts. Top with the remaining bread and serve.

5. This sandwich would also be delicious on sourdough bread, and you can use the leftover yogurt mixture as a salad dressing or for more sandwiches.

Substitution Tip: Tarragon is a delicious replacement if dill is not available. You can also substitute vegan mayo for the Greek yogurt.

PER SERVING: Calories: 388; Total fat: 25g; Total carbs: 37g; Fiber: 8g; Sugar: 9g; Protein: 14g; Sodium: 318mg

Roasted Eggplant Lasagna Rolls

DAIRY-FREE, GLUTEN-FREE, NUT-FREE, 30-MINUTE, VEGAN

Eggplant lasagna tends to take longer than 30 minutes to make. I wondered how I could reduce the time but not the flavor. Then it hit me: eggplant rolls. If prepared correctly, eggplant, also known as aubergine, provides a slightly nutty yet mild flavor. Salt your raw eggplant before cooking it to extract water and remove its bitter taste.

Serves 4   **Prep time: 15 minutes / Cook time: 15 minutes**

1 eggplant, cut into
    ¼-inch-thick slices
Salt
1 (14-ounce) block tofu
3 tablespoons
    nutritional yeast
Juice of 1 lemon
1 tablespoon
    dried oregano
½ cup fresh basil
    (optional)
Freshly ground
    black pepper
1 cup marinara sauce

1. Preheat the oven to 425°F.

2. Arrange the eggplant slices on a baking sheet, salt them lightly, and bake for 10 minutes. Remove from the oven and let cool slightly.

3. Meanwhile, in a food processor, combine the tofu, nutritional yeast, lemon juice, oregano, basil (if using), and a pinch each of salt and pepper. Pulse for 12 seconds, scraping down the sides as needed. You want a semi-pureed mixture with a consistency similar to ricotta. Taste and adjust the seasoning as needed.

4. Line the bottom of a baking dish with ½ cup of marinara sauce.

5. Scoop approximately 2 tablespoons of the tofu ricotta mixture onto the end of each eggplant slice. Gently roll up the eggplant slices and place each roll facedown in the sauce in the baking dish.

6. Pour the remaining ½ cup of marinara sauce over the eggplant rolls.

7. Bake for 15 minutes, or until the eggplant is lightly browned.

8. Serve immediately. This dish is best served fresh but you can store it, covered, in the refrigerator overnight to enjoy the following day.

Meal-Prep Tip: Make extra tofu ricotta; it will keep in the refrigerator for up to 4 days and is great in sandwiches and wraps or on pasta.

PER SERVING: Calories: 156; Total fat: 5g; Total carbs: 19g; Fiber: 10g; Sugar: 7g; Protein: 15g; Sodium: 338mg

Rustic Fish Chowder

DAIRY-FREE, GLUTEN-FREE, NUT-FREE, ONE POT

This fish chowder has a hint of sweetness thanks to corn. Frozen or canned corn works great, but I love to use fresh corn—just use a large knife to scrape the kernels off the cob, then add them to the soup. The chowder is delicious served with fresh bread to dunk into the broth.

Serves 4   **Prep time: 15 minutes / Cook time: 25 minutes**

2 pounds cod (or any white-fleshed fish)
3 tablespoons olive oil
4 garlic cloves, minced
2 tomatoes, chopped
2 celery stalks, chopped
4 cups vegetable broth
Salt
Freshly ground black pepper
1 ear fresh corn, cut into chunks

1. Rinse the fish under cold running water for 5 minutes. Let dry, then cut into chunks.

2. In a large pot, heat the olive oil over medium heat. Add the garlic and cook for 3 minutes, until it is light brown.

3. Add the tomatoes and celery and cook for 5 minutes.

4. Slowly add the chunks of fish to the pot, stirring frequently.

5. Pour in the broth, bring to a boil, and then reduce the heat and simmer, covered, for 10 minutes. Season with salt and pepper. Serve immediately, with chunks of corn.

Meal-Prep Tip: Make extra chowder to store in the refrigerator for a lovely lunch the next day. You can serve leftovers over potatoes or a bed of rice.

PER SERVING: Calories: 317; Total fat: 13g; Total carbs: 10g; Fiber: 2g; Sugar: 4g; Protein: 41g; Sodium: 681mg

Zucchini Pasta with Tomato Marinara

5-INGREDIENT, GLUTEN-FREE, NUT-FREE, ONE POT, 30-MINUTE, VEGETARIAN

This recipe is a wonderful way to eat "pasta" without the carbs for a light dinner. A spiralizer creates perfect spaghetti-shaped zoodles. If you don't have a spiralizer, you can use a julienne peeler instead. You don't need to boil zoodles; simply sauté them briefly in olive oil.

Serves 2   **Prep time: 10 minutes / Cook time: 20 minutes**

3 zucchini
3 tablespoons olive oil, divided
2 garlic cloves, minced
2 tomatoes, diced
1 (24-ounce) jar marinara sauce
Grated Parmesan cheese, for serving

1. Spiralize the zucchini into zoodles. Set aside.

2. In a large skillet, heat 2 tablespoons of olive oil over medium heat. Add the garlic and cook for 4 minutes.

3. Add the zoodles and cook for 2 minutes (they do not take long). Remove from the pan and set aside.

4. Add the remaining 1 tablespoon of olive oil to the pan, toss in the tomatoes, and cook for 4 minutes.

5. Add the marinara sauce to the pan and cook for 3 minutes.

6. Return the zoodles to the pan and stir to coat the zoodles with the sauce. Remove from the heat, sprinkle with Parmesan, and serve immediately.

Prep Tip: Discard the mushier zoodles that come from the zucchini core.

PER SERVING: Calories: 335; Total fat: 22g; Total carbs: 34g; Fiber: 10g; Sugar: 23g; Protein: 9g; Sodium: 1,819mg

Summer Squash Tacos with Citrus-Marinated Tilapia

GLUTEN-FREE, NUT-FREE, ONE POT

These summer tacos pack just the right amount of heat. The citrus marinade gives the tilapia a zesty flavor. Tilapia is available fresh or frozen and is a great mild-flavored fish that works perfectly for tacos. The summer squash pairs beautifully and adds nutrients like vitamin A and C as well as omega-3 fatty acids and minerals.

Serves 2   **Prep time: 20 minutes / Cook time: 15 minutes**

5 tablespoons olive oil, divided

3 chipotle chiles, minced

Juice of 3 lemons

2 teaspoons ground cumin

2 pounds tilapia fillets

2 summer squash, cut into ½-inch-thick slices

2 zucchini, cut into ½-inch-thick slices

Salt

Freshly ground black pepper

½ cup plain Greek yogurt

6 corn tortillas

1 avocado, pitted, peeled, and sliced

Fresh cilantro, for garnish (optional)

1. In a bowl, stir together 1 tablespoon of olive oil, the chipotle chiles, 2 tablespoons of lemon juice, and cumin. Add the tilapia fillets to the bowl and ladle the marinade over the fillets, coating them completely. Refrigerate for 15 minutes.

2. In a medium-size skillet, heat 2 tablespoons of olive oil over medium heat. Add the summer squash and zucchini and season with salt and pepper. Cook for 6 minutes. Remove from the heat and set aside.

3. In the same pan, heat the remaining 2 tablespoons of olive oil over medium heat. Place the tilapia fillets in the pan. Cook for 5 minutes per side, or until the fish is opaque and flakes easily with a fork. Squeeze the juice of 1 lemon onto the fish while cooking. Remove from the heat and cut the fish into chunks.

CONTINUED

4. In a small bowl, stir together the yogurt and the remaining 2 tablespoons of lemon juice, and season with salt and pepper.

5. Heat the tortillas in the skillet, working in batches as needed. Divide the fish and vegetables among the tortillas and top with the yogurt mixture and avocado slices. Garnish with fresh cilantro (if using), and serve immediately.

Shopping Tip: When you're buying summer squash, make sure to choose bright ones. You don't want to see any spots or bruising.

PER SERVING: Calories: 650; Total fat: 33g; Total carbs: 32g; Fiber: 8g; Sugar: 8g; Protein: 67g; Sodium: 176mg

Okra Coconut Curry

DAIRY-FREE, GLUTEN-FREE, VEGAN

Okra curry is a popular curry in Southeast Asia. Tomatoes, coconut cream, and curry spices combine to create a perfect flavor profile for summer. You can eat this curry on its own or with white or brown rice. Okra contains vitamins K and C, B vitamins, and fiber. This recipe calls for green curry paste, which you can find in the international aisle of grocery stores. If it's not available, red will work instead. (If you can't find either, the turmeric will suffice.)

Serves 4   **Prep time: 15 minutes / Cook time: 20 minutes**

2 pounds okra, halved

3 tomatoes, chopped

4 ounces green curry paste

1 (13.5-ounce) can coconut cream

½ cup vegetable broth

1 teaspoon ground turmeric

Pinch salt

Pinch freshly ground black pepper

Cooked rice, for serving

1. In a large pot, cook the okra over medium heat for 4 minutes. (Do not add any oil.)

2. Add the tomatoes and curry paste and cook, stirring, for 2 minutes.

3. While stirring, slowly pour in the coconut cream and the broth. Add the turmeric, salt, and pepper and stir. Turn the heat to low, cover, and cook for 12 minutes.

4. Serve with rice. You can store leftovers in an airtight container in the refrigerator for up to 1 day.

Prep Tip: Okra can get a little slimy when cooking with liquid, so cook it with dry heat to get it crispy.

PER SERVING: Calories: 392; Total fat: 28g; Total carbs: 31g; Fiber: 9g; Sugar: 6g; Protein: 8g; Sodium: 1,113mg

Paella with Shrimp, Bell Peppers, and Corn

DAIRY-FREE, NUT-FREE, ONE POT

Popular in Spain, this dish traditionally uses seafood, but you can add a different protein, such as a chicken sausage, if you'd like. This quick-and-easy shareable dish is perfect party fare.

Serves 6   **Prep time: 15 minutes / Cook time: 40 minutes**

¼ cup olive oil, plus more
   if needed
5 garlic cloves, minced
1 red bell pepper, diced
1 orange bell
   pepper, diced
2 large tomatoes, diced
1 cup uncooked white rice
2 cups vegetable broth
½ teaspoon
   saffron threads
2 teaspoons
   smoked paprika
8 ounces shrimp, peeled,
   deveined, and rinsed
½ (15-ounce) can
   corn kernels
Salt
Freshly ground
   black pepper
1 lemon, halved
Chopped fresh parsley,
   for garnish
Baguette, for serving

1. In a large pot, heat the olive oil over medium-high heat. Add the garlic and cook for 3 minutes, or until light brown. Add the bell peppers and cook for 3 minutes.

2. Add the tomatoes and cook for 2 minutes. Add more olive oil if needed.

3. Add the rice and stir to combine. Cook for 3 minutes.

4. Slowly pour in 1 cup of the broth and add the saffron and paprika. Bring to a boil, then stir in the remainder of the broth and bring back to a boil. Reduce the heat to maintain a simmer, cover, and cook for 15 minutes.

5. Add the shrimp. Cover again and cook for 7 minutes more, or until the broth is fully absorbed into the rice and the shrimp have turned pink.

6. Top with the corn and season with salt and pepper.

7. Squeeze the lemon over the shrimp and garnish with parsley. Serve with a fresh baguette.

Prep Tip: Paella recipes typically call for a special paella pan, but don't worry if you don't have one (most people outside Spain don't). A stockpot will work just fine for this recipe.

PER SERVING: Calories: 280; Total fat: 11g; Total carbs: 36g; Fiber: 3g; Sugar: 4g; Protein: 12g; Sodium: 270mg

Miso Eggplant with Basil

5-INGREDIENT, NUT-FREE, 30-MINUTE, VEGAN

Eggplant can hold its own in most recipes. It is delicious in curries, stir-fries, and Italian food, and it boasts a pretty impressive nutrient profile. Packed with B vitamins, which promote healthy nerve function, it also has a large amount of vitamin K, which is great for bone and blood health.

Serves 2   **Prep time: 10 minutes / Cook time: 20 minutes**

2 large eggplant, halved lengthwise
Salt
½ cup miso paste
3 teaspoons soy sauce
1 teaspoon white vinegar
2 teaspoons toasted sesame oil
Cooked rice, for serving

1. Preheat the oven to 425°F. Line a baking sheet with parchment paper.

2. Place the eggplants on the prepared sheet. Sprinkle salt over the eggplant halves. Roast for 15 minutes.

3. While the eggplant is roasting, in a bowl, whisk together the miso paste, soy sauce, and vinegar.

4. Remove the eggplant from the oven and slather the eggplant slices with the miso mixture. Move the baking rack up toward the top of the oven and turn the oven to broil. Broil for 4 minutes, or until the miso crust is caramelized.

5. Remove the eggplant from the oven and top with sesame oil. Serve immediately with rice.

Meal-Prep Tip: The eggplant slices also make for a delicious sandwich with sprouts and lettuce.

PER SERVING: Calories: 319; Total fat: 10g; Total carbs: 51g; Fiber: 23g; Sugar: 21g; Protein: 14g; Sodium: 3,022mg

Vegan Spicy Tuna Avocado Roll

DAIRY-FREE, NUT-FREE, 30-MINUTE, VEGAN

This recipe calls for sushi rice, which you can find at the grocery store or online. Avocado adds a healthy fat, which leaves you feeling full. Adjust the sriracha as desired.

Serves 2 **Prep time: 10 minutes / Cook time: 15 minutes**

1 cup uncooked sushi rice
2 tablespoons rice vinegar, divided
½ teaspoon salt
6 tomatoes
3 tablespoons soy sauce
1 teaspoon kelp powder (optional)
½ tablespoon sriracha
1 tablespoon toasted sesame oil
1 cucumber, peeled and thinly sliced
1 avocado, pitted, peeled, and thinly sliced

1. Combine 2 cups water and the sushi rice in a medium pot and bring to a boil. Cover and reduce the heat to maintain a simmer. Cook for 15 minutes, until the water has been absorbed. Add 1 tablespoon of vinegar and the salt and stir to combine. Set aside.

2. Bring a large pot of water to a boil. Fill a large bowl with ice and water. Add the tomatoes to the boiling water and cook for 5 minutes, or until their skins begin to peel off. Transfer to the ice water and let cool.

3. In a shallow bowl with a sealable lid, whisk together the soy sauce, remaining 1 tablespoon of vinegar, kelp powder (if using), sriracha, and sesame oil.

4. Peel the tomatoes, then slice each into 3 vertical slices and remove the seeds. Place the tomato slices into the sauce so they are fully submerged. Let sit for at least 10 minutes.

5. Shape the rice into 10 to 15 small balls. Remove a tomato slice from the marinade and lay it over each ball. Top with cucumber and avocado.

Meal-Prep Tip: Make and store extra sauce in an airtight container for up to 5 days.

PER SERVING: Calories: 629; Total fat: 21g; Total carbs: 104g; Fiber: 11g; Sugar: 13g; Protein: 13g; Sodium: 1,962mg

Tomato Caprese Burgers

GLUTEN-FREE, NUT-FREE, 30-MINUTE, VEGETARIAN

This raw caprese "burger" is perfect for a picnic. When choosing tomatoes for the recipe, opt for those on the firmer side.

Serves 2 **Prep time: 10 minutes**

3 tomatoes, cut into
  ½-inch-thick slices
2 tablespoons
  balsamic vinegar
2 tablespoons olive oil
Salt
Freshly ground
  black pepper
8 ounces fresh mozzarella
  cheese, sliced
½ cup fresh basil

1. Put the tomato slices on a large plate and drizzle with the vinegar and olive oil. Sprinkle with salt and pepper.

2. Arrange the salad on a serving plate: Layer one slice of mozzarella, then a tomato slice, basil leaf, mozzarella slice, basil leaf, and tomato slice.

3. Season with a pinch each of salt and pepper and serve immediately.

Prep Tip: You can throw the tomato slices on the grill to get a delicious seared flavor.

PER SERVING: Calories: 518; Total fat: 38g; Total carbs: 8g; Fiber: 2g; Sugar: 5g; Protein: 22g; Sodium: 530mg

Summer Harvest Stir-Fry

ONE POT, VEGAN

This stir-fry is a great way to use up veggies in your refrigerator that are approaching the end of their life. Top it off with toasted cashews for a satisfying crunch.

Serves 2   **Prep time: 15 minutes / Cook time: 20 minutes**

3 tablespoons olive oil
3 garlic cloves, minced
1 carrot, diced
1 celery stalk, chopped
½ eggplant, cubed
8 ounces green beans
½ (13.5-ounce)
   coconut cream
2 tablespoons
   nutritional yeast
2 tablespoons soy sauce
1 teaspoon cornstarch
Salt
Freshly ground
   black pepper

1. In a large skillet, heat the olive oil over medium heat.

2. Add the garlic and cook for 3 minutes. Add the carrot, celery, eggplant, and green beans. Cook for 7 minutes, stirring frequently.

3. Slowly pour in the coconut cream.

4. Add the nutritional yeast, soy sauce, and cornstarch to thicken the mixture. Stir to combine. Cover and cook for 6 minutes.

5. Season with salt and pepper and serve immediately. You can store leftovers in an airtight container in the refrigerator for up to 1 day.

Prep Tip: Mince extra garlic and store in a jar in the refrigerator to use in future recipes.

PER SERVING: Calories: 610; Total fat: 35g; Total carbs: 70g; Fiber: 13g; Sugar: 46g; Protein: 14g; Sodium: 1,049mg

CREAMY LEEK AND
POTATO SOUP
PAGE 81

4

chapter four fall
September Through November

Fall is the time for winter squash, mushrooms, cauliflower, collard greens, and Brussels sprouts.

Sweet Potato, Tomato, and Carrot Soup

NUT-FREE, VEGAN

This recipe spices up tomato soup. Sweet potato and carrot have a similarly sweet flavor, and when combined, they taste amazing.

Serves 2   **Prep time: 10 minutes / Cook time: 25 minutes**

1 sweet potato, halved
  and peeled
2 carrots
3 tomatoes
1 small piece fresh
  ginger, peeled
½ cup vegetable broth
Salt
Freshly ground
  black pepper
Toasted bread, for serving

1. Preheat the oven to 400°F. Line a baking dish with parchment paper.

2. Place the sweet potato, carrots, and tomatoes on the prepared sheet. Bake for 20 minutes. Remove from the oven and let cool slightly.

3. When cool enough to handle, scoop the sweet potato flesh into a blender. Add the carrots, tomatoes, ginger, and broth. Blend on high speed for 1 minute, or until smooth.

4. Transfer the contents of the blender to a pot and cook over medium heat for 5 minutes, until heated through.

5. Season with salt and pepper and serve with a delicious piece of toast.

Time-Saving Tip: Purchase prechopped sweet potatoes to cut down your prep time.

PER SERVING: Calories: 124; Total fat: 1g; Total carbs: 27g; Fiber: 6g; Sugar: 11g; Protein: 4g; Sodium: 355mg

Butternut Squash Soup with Apple

DAIRY-FREE, 5-INGREDIENT, GLUTEN-FREE, NUT-FREE, VEGAN

This soup is convenient, nutritious, and a delight to enjoy in the fall.

Serves 2   Prep time: 10 minutes / Cook time: 30 minutes

1 large butternut squash,
   halved and seeded
3 tablespoons olive oil
1 small onion, chopped
½ cup vegetable broth
½ small apple, cored
   and sliced
Salt
Freshly ground
   black pepper

1. Preheat the oven to 400°F.
2. Place the butternut squash in a baking dish and bake for 25 minutes, or until tender.
3. While the squash roasts, in a medium skillet, heat the olive oil over medium-low heat. Add the onion and cook for 4 minutes.
4. Scoop out the flesh of the roasted squash and place it in a blender. Add the onion, broth, and apple and blend on high speed for 1 minute, or until smooth.
5. Season with salt and pepper and serve immediately.

Shopping Tip: When you purchase squash, it should be beige in color and have a matte appearance. Waxy or shiny skin means it's not yet ripe.

PER SERVING: Calories: 416; Total fat: 22g; Total carbs: 61g; Fiber: 11g; Sugar: 17g; Protein: 5g; Sodium: 229mg

Oven-Roasted Cauliflower and Turmeric Soup

DAIRY-FREE, GLUTEN-FREE, VEGAN

Turmeric gives this soup a beautiful gold color, and cauliflower adds creaminess. Garnish this soup with walnuts and sunflower seeds, and serve with fresh bread.

Serves 4 **Prep time: 15 minutes / Cook time: 20 minutes**

2 heads cauliflower, chopped into florets

1 yellow onion, diced

3 tablespoons olive oil

3 teaspoons turmeric, divided

Pinch salt

Pinch freshly ground black pepper

2 cups vegetable broth

1 cup coconut milk

1 teaspoon smoked paprika

1 teaspoon ground cumin

½ cup frozen sweet peas

½ cup walnuts, chopped (optional)

½ cup sunflower seeds (optional)

1. Preheat the oven to 400°F. Line a large rimmed baking sheet with parchment paper.

2. Place the cauliflower and onion on the prepared sheet. Drizzle with olive oil and 1½ teaspoons of turmeric. Season with salt and pepper.

3. Bake for 10 minutes. While the cauliflower is baking, pour the vegetable broth and coconut milk into a blender.

4. Add the roasted cauliflower and onion to the blender and blend on high speed until smooth.

5. Transfer the mixture to a pot and bring to a simmer. Add the remaining 1½ teaspoons of turmeric, paprika, and cumin.

6. While simmering, add the sweet peas. Continue simmering for 2 minutes.

7. Garnish with chopped walnuts or sunflower seeds (if using) and serve immediately.

Shopping Tip: When purchasing cauliflower, make sure the head is a nice off-white color and has no dark spots.

PER SERVING: Calories: 269; Total fat: 23g; Total carbs: 15g; Fiber: 6g; Sugar: 6g; Protein: 5g; Sodium: 225mg

Creamy Leek and Potato Soup

GLUTEN-FREE, ONE POT, VEGETARIAN

Leeks, which are high in fiber, minerals, and B vitamins, make this French classic nutrient dense. Potatoes and coconut milk provide a creamy consistency. You can replace the coconut milk with any nonsweetened plant-based milk.

Serves 4   **Prep time: 15 minutes / Cook time: 30 minutes**

2 tablespoons olive oil

1 tablespoon butter

1 onion, diced

3 garlic cloves

3 leeks, cleaned and
   thinly sliced

5 potatoes, peeled
   and chopped

1 rosemary sprig

1 teaspoon dried thyme

4 cups vegetable broth

1 (13.5-ounce) can
   coconut cream

Juice of 1 lemon

Salt

Freshly ground black
   pepper, plus more
   for garnish

Roasted potatoes or
   bread, for serving
   (optional)

Chopped scallions, for
   garnish (optional)

1. In a large skillet, heat the olive oil and butter over medium heat. Add the onion and garlic and cook for 4 minutes, or until the onion is translucent.

2. Add the leeks and cook for 4 minutes.

3. Add the potatoes and cook for 3 minutes.

4. Add the rosemary and thyme and cook for 3 minutes. Pour in the vegetable broth and coconut cream. Bring to a boil, add the lemon juice, and season with salt and pepper.

5. Cover and simmer for 15 minutes, or until the potatoes are soft.

6. Transfer the mixture to a blender and blend on high speed for up to 1 minute, or until smooth.

7. Garnish with scallions and more freshly ground pepper (if using). Serve with roasted potatoes or bread (if using). This soup freezes great, so you can store leftovers in an airtight container in the freezer for up to 3 months.

Substitution Tip: Instead of butter, you can use coconut oil, vegan butter, or more olive oil to make this recipe vegan and dairy free.

PER SERVING: Calories: 718; Total fat: 28g; Total carbs: 114g; Fiber: 10g; Sugar: 63g; Protein: 7g; Sodium: 660mg

Biscuit Chickpea Potpie

This potpie is the very definition of comfort food. Each bite is a perfect balance of juicy biscuit, savory vegetables, and protein-packed chickpeas. And unlike many potpies, it won't leave you feeling uncomfortably full.

Serves 4 **Prep time: 15 minutes / Cook time: 30 minutes**

2 tablespoons olive oil

1 yellow onion, chopped

2 cups vegetable broth

2½ cups unsweetened nondairy milk, divided

2⅓ cups all-purpose or gluten-free flour, divided

3 cups frozen mixed vegetables

1 russet potato, peeled and finely chopped

1 (15-ounce) can chickpeas, drained and rinsed

1 tablespoon baking powder

1 teaspoon salt

8 tablespoons (1 stick) butter, melted

2 tablespoons nutritional yeast

1. Preheat the oven to 400°F.

2. In a medium skillet, heat the olive oil over medium heat. Add the onion and sauté for 4 minutes.

3. Pour in the broth and 1½ cups of milk, and whisk in ⅓ cup of flour to thicken. Whisk until smooth.

4. Add the vegetables, potato, and chickpeas. Simmer until the sauce thickens.

5. Transfer the filling to a large baking dish.

6. In a large bowl, combine the remaining 2 cups of flour, the baking powder, salt, melted butter, remaining 1 cup of milk, and nutritional yeast. Mix until a dough forms.

7. Using a spoon, scoop up small amounts of the dough and dollop them over the filling. The dough should not completely cover the filling.

8. Bake for 20 minutes, or until the biscuits are browned. Remove from the oven and serve immediately.

Prep Tip: When you dollop the dough onto the filling, a little goes a long way. Use smaller scoops.

Time-Saving Tip: To make this recipe even easier, use store-bought biscuits. Bake the filling for 10 minutes, top with store-bought dough, and bake for 10 minutes more.

PER SERVING: Calories: 833; Total fat: 36g; Total carbs: 106g; Fiber: 22g; Sugar: 11g; Protein: 27g; Sodium: 1,118mg

Lasagna with Tofu Ricotta

DAIRY-FREE, ONE POT, VEGAN

This lasagna is sure to please. Carrots, spinach, and Swiss chard add healthy vitamins and minerals like iron, vitamin A, and vitamin C. Trust me on adding the tofu ricotta; several cheese lovers have given it the stamp of approval. The consistency is pretty much identical to ricotta, and the oregano and nutritional yeast create the same flavor profile. (The secret is oregano.)

Serves 4   **Prep time: 20 minutes / Cook time: 35 minutes**

1 box lasagna noodles
2 (9-ounce) jars marinara sauce
2 carrots, chopped
1 cup raw cashews
1 (14-ounce) block tofu
2 tablespoons nutritional yeast
2 teaspoons dried oregano
Juice of 1 lemon
1 teaspoon salt
3 cups baby spinach
2 cups chopped Swiss chard

1. Preheat the oven to 375°F.

2. Bring a large pot of water to a boil. Add the noodles and cook according to the package instructions. Drain and rinse the noodles, then set aside.

3. In a large skillet, heat the marinara sauce over medium heat. Add the carrots. Cover and simmer for 5 to 7 minutes, until the carrots are on the softer side. Set aside.

4. In a food processor, combine the cashews, tofu, nutritional yeast, oregano, lemon juice, and salt. Pulse for 30 to 45 seconds, until the mixture resembles ricotta.

5. Spread 1 cup of marinara sauce over the bottom of a 9-by-13-inch casserole dish. Add a layer of noodles. Spread a layer of the tofu ricotta mixture on top of the noodles, then top with some of the spinach and chard. Add another layer of marinara sauce over the greens, then top with a layer of the lasagna noodles. Spread the rest of the tofu ricotta over the noodles and top with the remaining greens. Place a final layer of noodles on top of the greens and pour the remaining marinara sauce over the noodles.

6. Bake for 25 minutes, until the lasagna has melted together. Let cool before serving. You can store leftovers in an airtight container in the refrigerator for up to 2 days.

Prep Tip: Replace the cashews with almonds for the tofu ricotta. You can also swap the cashews for 6 ounces of mushrooms and a can of drained chickpeas.

PER SERVING: Calories: 689; Total fat: 27g; Total carbs: 83g; Fiber: 7g; Sugar: 10g; Protein: 32g; Sodium: 1,484mg

Quinoa and Cranberry–Stuffed Acorn Squash

DAIRY-FREE, NUT-FREE, VEGAN

This lovely meal would be a great addition to any Thanksgiving dinner. The stuffing is savory and pairs perfectly with the squash. The maple syrup and dried cranberries add sweetness and tanginess to the recipe. As a topping, try Spicy Cashew Cheese (page 143).

Serves 4 · **Prep time: 15 minutes / Cook time: 55 minutes**

1 cup quinoa, rinsed

2 acorn squash, halved and seeded

2 tablespoons olive oil, plus more for drizzling

1 teaspoon maple syrup, plus more for drizzling

Salt

Freshly ground black pepper

1 onion, finely chopped

1 celery stalk, finely chopped

½ (14-ounce) block tofu, crumbled

¼ cup dried cranberries

1. Preheat the oven to 425°F.

2. In a medium pot, bring 2 cups water with the quinoa to a boil over medium-high heat. When the water reaches a boil, cover and reduce the heat to maintain a simmer. Cook for 15 minutes, or until the quinoa is tender. Fluff it with a fork and set aside.

3. Place the squash halves cut-side up on a sheet pan and drizzle with olive oil and the maple syrup. Season with salt and pepper.

4. In a medium skillet, heat the olive oil over medium heat. Add the onion and cook for 3 to 4 minutes, until translucent. Add the celery and cook for 4 minutes.

5. Add the quinoa, tofu, and cranberries to the skillet and cook for 5 minutes.

6. Stuff the squash halves with the filling and bake for 35 minutes, until the edges of the squash begin to brown.

7. Drizzle with maple syrup, season with salt and pepper, and serve immediately.

PER SERVING: Calories: 383; Total fat: 13g; Total carbs: 60g; Fiber: 8g; Sugar: 7g; Protein: 13g; Sodium: 68mg

Glazed Hasselback Sweet Potato with Brussels Sprouts

DAIRY-FREE, 5-INGREDIENT, GLUTEN-FREE, NUT-FREE, ONE POT, VEGAN

Hasselback potatoes can be made from white potatoes or sweet potatoes—or both! Sweet potatoes provide sweetness, whereas Yukon Gold potatoes are super creamy. The Brussels sprouts add a beautiful pop of color and more fiber to the meal. To prep the Brussels sprouts, trim off the stem end and peel off the first layer of leaves.

Serves 4 **Prep time: 15 minutes / Cook time: 35 minutes**

4 small sweet potatoes

4 small Yukon Gold or russet potatoes

8 ounces Brussels sprouts, halved

¼ cup olive oil

1 teaspoon salt

½ teaspoon freshly ground black pepper

3 rosemary sprigs

1. Preheat the oven to 400°F.

2. Working with one potato at a time and using a sharp knife, cut crosswise almost all the way through the potato from top to bottom, then continue to make cuts down the length of the potato.

3. Place the potatoes on a baking sheet along with the Brussels sprouts.

4. Drizzle with the olive oil, season with the salt and pepper, and top off with the rosemary.

5. Bake for 35 minutes, or until the potatoes are soft. Serve immediately. These are best served fresh, but you can store leftovers in the refrigerator overnight.

Prep Tip: The sweet potatoes can be peeled or unpeeled for this recipe.

Shopping Tip: Purchase sweet potatoes that are roughly equal in size and shape and have undamaged skin.

PER SERVING: Calories: 374; Total fat: 14g; Total carbs: 58g; Fiber: 10g; Sugar: 9g; Protein: 7g; Sodium: 677mg

Pumpkin Risotto with Arugula

DAIRY-FREE, GLUTEN-FREE, NUT-FREE, ONE POT, VEGAN

Risotto is a creamy rice dish that is popular in Italy. It calls for Arborio rice, a short-grain variety that absorbs a lot of broth. Canned pumpkin puree adds convenience, flavor, nutrients, and a hint of fall to this recipe. Top with freshly grated Parmesan cheese to make it really authentic.

Serves 4   **Prep time: 15 minutes / Cook time: 30 minutes**

2 tablespoons olive oil
1 small onion,
   finely chopped
2 garlic cloves, minced
1 cup Arborio rice
3 cups vegetable
   broth, divided
1 (15-ounce) can pure
   pumpkin puree
1 teaspoon salt
Pinch freshly
   ground pepper
Fresh sage, for seasoning
   (optional)

1. In a medium skillet, heat the olive oil over medium heat. Add the onion and garlic and cook for 4 minutes.

2. Add the rice to the skillet and stir to coat with the oil. Cook for 3 minutes, stirring frequently.

3. Slowly pour in 1 cup of broth. Bring to a boil, then reduce the heat to maintain a simmer. Cook, stirring frequently, until the rice has absorbed all the liquid.

4. Add another 1 cup of the broth and cook, stirring frequently, until it has been absorbed, then repeat with the final 1 cup broth. Cook until the rice is tender, about 15 minutes.

5. Add the pumpkin puree and stir. Season with salt and pepper. Stir in some fresh sage (if using) and serve immediately.

Prep Tip: If you'd like to add meat, shrimp always goes well with any risotto meal.

PER SERVING: Calories: 277; Total fat: 7g; Total carbs: 48g; Fiber: 4g; Sugar: 4g; Protein: 4g; Sodium: 988mg

Couscous with Rosemary and Garlic Mushrooms

DAIRY-FREE, NUT-FREE, 30-MINUTE, VEGAN

A rice alternative, couscous is extremely fluffy and pairs well with the umami flavor of mushrooms. Many mushrooms are in season during fall, so pick up your favorite or whatever is featured at your local market.

Serves 2   **Prep time: 10 minutes / Cook time: 15 minutes**

1 cup uncooked couscous
2 cups vegetable broth
¼ cup olive oil
4 garlic cloves, minced
2 rosemary sprigs
8 ounces
   mushrooms, sliced
Pinch salt
Pinch freshly ground
   black pepper
2 cups spinach

1. In a medium pot, combine the couscous and broth and bring to a boil, then reduce the heat to low, cover, and simmer for 12 minutes, or until the couscous has absorbed all the liquid. Fluff the couscous and set aside.

2. In a separate pan, heat the olive oil over medium heat. Add the garlic and cook for 3 minutes, or until it begins to turn slightly brown.

3. Add the rosemary and cook for 3 minutes. Add the mushrooms, salt, and pepper and cook for 5 minutes. Add the spinach and cover. Cook for 1 minute, or until the spinach has wilted.

4. Remove the rosemary before serving. Serve the mushrooms on a bed of the couscous.

Prep Tip: To make a delicious rosemary-infused oil, combine ¼ cup olive oil with a few rosemary sprigs and cook on low heat for up to 20 minutes. Transfer to a bottle and store in a dark, cool spot.

PER SERVING: Calories: 644; Total fat: 30g; Total carbs: 75g; Fiber: 6g; Sugar: 3g; Protein: 21g; Sodium: 881mg

Fall Vegetable Roast

DAIRY-FREE, GLUTEN-FREE, NUT-FREE, VEGAN

This veggie roast is an incredibly easy way to use up your fall produce, especially the starchier ones, such as carrots, potatoes, parsnips, and yams. Cauliflower and onions work great, too. If you prepare this in a casserole dish, juice from the vegetables creates a delicious sauce, which tastes great on rice or even as a marinade.

Serves 4   **Prep time: 20 minutes / Cook time: 25 minutes**

3 carrots

3 tomatoes

2 onions

3 beets

2 garlic cloves, peeled

½ head cauliflower

6 small potatoes

5 tablespoons olive
oil, divided

1 teaspoon salt

Pinch freshly
ground pepper

1 teaspoon ground
turmeric

1 teaspoon
smoked paprika

1 teaspoon garlic powder

2 teaspoons maple syrup
(optional)

1. Preheat the oven to 400°F.

2. In a large pot, boil 2 quarts water. Coarsely chop the carrots, tomatoes, onions, beets, garlic, cauliflower, and potatoes and put them in the pot. Cook for 15 minutes, then drain all the water from the pot. Add 3 tablespoons of olive oil and the salt, pepper, turmeric, paprika, garlic powder, and maple syrup (if using) to the pot. Toss so the vegetables are well coated.

3. Transfer the vegetables to a 9-by-13-inch casserole dish and drizzle with the remaining 2 tablespoons of olive oil.

4. Bake for 20 to 25 minutes.

5. Serve with rice or even inside tortillas as tacos.

6. You can store leftovers covered in foil in the refrigerator for up to 1 day.

Meal-Prep Tip: This recipe's olive oil and spice mixture makes a great marinade for tofu, meat, fish, vegetables, and is even a great salad dressing. Double the amounts here and store half the mixture in a jar for up to 4 weeks.

PER SERVING: Calories: 433; Total fat: 18g; Total carbs: 64g; Fiber: 12g; Sugar: 17g; Protein: 8g; Sodium: 703mg

Creamy Polenta with Mushroom Gravy

DAIRY-FREE, 5-INGREDIENT, GLUTEN-FREE, NUT-FREE, 30-MINUTE, VEGAN

Polenta is a great alternative to pasta or potatoes. It is often made into cakes, but this recipe calls for a creamy version that tastes amazing with the savory mushroom gravy. It is great for a quick dinner or a special occasion.

Serves 2   **Prep time: 15 minutes / Cook time: 15 minutes**

2 (18-ounce) packages precooked polenta
1/2 cup vegetable broth, divided
1/2 teaspoon freshly ground black pepper
2 tablespoons olive oil
8 ounces mushrooms, sliced
1 teaspoon cornstarch
Pinch salt
1 bunch fresh parsley, chopped (optional)

1. Place the polenta and ¼ of cup vegetable broth in a food processor. Blend until smooth. Add the pepper.
2. Transfer the mixture to a small saucepan and heat over low heat.
3. In a medium skillet, heat the olive oil over medium heat. Add the mushrooms, the remaining ¼ cup of vegetable broth, and the cornstarch. Cook for 4 minutes. Add the salt.
4. Transfer the warmed polenta into a bowl, and top with the mushrooms and mushroom gravy.
5. Garnish with parsley (if using).

Time-Saving Tip: You can find precooked and packaged polenta at your grocery store in the pasta section or order it online.

PER SERVING: Calories: 468; Total fat: 14g; Total carbs: 73g; Fiber: 6g; Sugar: 7g; Protein: 13g; Sodium: 1,484mg

Lentil Shepherd's Pie

DAIRY-FREE, GLUTEN-FREE, VEGAN

Shepherd's pie usually calls for ground beef, but this recipe uses lentils and vegetables. Lentils are a nutrition powerhouse and full of fiber, which will leave you feeling full.

Serves 4   **Prep time: 15 minutes / Cook time: 50 minutes**

6 tablespoons olive oil, divided
6 Yukon Gold potatoes, peeled and cubed
¼ cup nondairy milk
Salt
Freshly ground black pepper
1 yellow onion, chopped
2 carrots, diced
8 ounces mushrooms, diced
1 celery stalk, diced
1½ cups cooked brown or green lentils
2 teaspoons tomato paste
1 cup vegetable broth

1. Preheat the oven to 400°F and drizzle 3 tablespoons of olive oil into a 9-by-13-inch casserole dish.

2. Bring 3 cups water to a boil in a medium pot. Add the potatoes and cook for 10 minutes, or until soft. Drain the potatoes and place in a bowl. Mash with a fork, adding the milk. Season with salt and pepper. Set aside.

3. In a medium pot, heat the remaining 3 tablespoons of olive oil over medium heat. Add the onion and cook for 4 minutes, or until translucent. Add the carrots, mushrooms, and celery and cook for 7 minutes. Add the cooked lentils, tomato paste, and vegetable broth. Bring to a boil, reduce the heat, and simmer for 5 minutes until the broth is absorbed.

4. Spread the filling evenly on the bottom of the casserole dish and top with the mashed potato mixture.

5. Bake for up to 20 minutes. All the ingredients are fully cooked, but this step allows the flavors to fully meld.

6. Season with additional salt and pepper, if needed, and serve immediately.

   Time-Saving Tip: For the sake of convenience, this recipe uses cooked lentils, which you can purchase at most grocery stores and online markets. If you can't find them, use uncooked lentils. Place them in 6 cups of boiling water, reduce the heat to a simmer, and cook, covered, for 15 minutes, until all the water is absorbed.

PER SERVING: Calories: 705; Total fat: 23g; Total carbs: 103g; Fiber: 32g; Sugar: 10g; Protein: 27g; Sodium: 234mg

Cabbage and Gnocchi

DAIRY-FREE, 5-INGREDIENT, NUT-FREE, VEGAN

This eastern European favorite is modernized with the addition of Brussels sprouts and gnocchi (bite-size dumplings made out of potatoes; you can find them in the pasta section of your grocery store). The cabbage provides tanginess.

Serves 2   **Prep time: 15 minutes / Cook time: 20 minutes**

3 tablespoons olive oil

1 head green cabbage, shredded

8 Brussels sprouts heads

1 cup vegetable broth

2 tablespoons white vinegar

Salt

Freshly ground black pepper

1 (12-ounce) box gnocchi

1. In a medium pot, heat the olive oil over medium heat. Add the shredded cabbage and Brussels sprouts heads and cook for 4 minutes.

2. Slowly pour in the vegetable broth and vinegar, then season with salt and pepper.

3. Cover and let simmer for 15 minutes.

4. In another pot, boil a small amount of water. Add the gnocchi and lower the heat. Cook for 7 minutes, or until the gnocchi float to the top. Drain the gnocchi.

5. Divide the cabbage and Brussels sprouts between two bowls and top with the gnocchi. Serve immediately. You can freeze leftovers in an airtight container in the freezer for up to 3 days.

Time-Saving Tip: You can purchase shredded cabbage in the produce section of the grocery store.

PER SERVING: Calories: 589; Total fat: 23g; Total carbs: 87g; Fiber: 19g; Sugar: 17g; Protein: 14g; Sodium: 1,421mg

Broccoli and Kale Chowder

DAIRY-FREE, GLUTEN-FREE, 30-MINUTE, VEGAN

This recipe calls for kale and broccoli, but you can use other leafy greens. Serve this chowder with grilled potatoes or a crunchy baguette.

Serves 2   **Prep time: 10 minutes / Cook time: 20 minutes**

3 tablespoons olive oil
1 small onion, chopped
2 broccoli heads
8 kale leaves, chopped
½ cup vegetable broth
½ cup coconut cream
Pinch salt
Pinch freshly ground
    black pepper

1. In a medium skillet, heat the olive oil over medium heat. Add the onion and cook for 4 minutes, or until translucent.

2. Add the broccoli and cook for 5 minutes more, until soft. Add the kale and cook for 4 minutes.

3. Transfer the mixture to a blender. Add the vegetable broth, coconut cream, salt, and pepper.

4. Blend on high speed until smooth.

5. Transfer the mixture into a pot and cook over medium heat for 4 minutes.

6. Serve immediately.

Time-Saving Tip: Buy broccoli florets to cut down on prep time.

PER SERVING: Calories: 489; Total fat: 30g; Total carbs: 51g; Fiber: 9g; Sugar: 32g; Protein: 11g; Sodium: 392mg

Garlic and Brussels Sprout Pasta

DAIRY-FREE, ONE POT, VEGETARIAN

This one-pot pasta satisfies any craving for cheese with a combination of vegetable broth, coconut cream, and nutritional yeast. The Brussels sprouts add sweetness, and the lemon juice provides a bit of tang.

Serves 2   **Prep time: 10 minutes / Cook time: 30 minutes**

4 tablespoons olive
  oil, divided
5 garlic cloves, minced
1 pound Brussels
  sprouts, halved
2½ cups vegetable broth
1 tablespoon
  nutritional yeast
1 (16-ounce) box angel
  hair pasta
1 cup coconut cream
Juice of 1 lemon
Salt
Freshly ground
  black pepper
½ cup grated
  Parmesan cheese

1. In a large pot, heat 2 tablespoons of olive oil over medium heat. Add the garlic and cook for 4 minutes, or until light brown.

2. Add the Brussels sprouts and cook for 7 minutes. The leaves should turn light brown and begin to look crispy. Remove the Brussels sprouts and set aside.

3. In the same pot, heat the remaining 2 tablespoons of olive oil. Add the vegetable broth and nutritional yeast and bring to a boil.

4. Once boiling, add the pasta and bring back to a boil. Reduce the heat to low and bring to a simmer. Cover and let simmer for 9 minutes, or until the liquid is absorbed.

5. Pour in the coconut cream and stir.

CONTINUED

6. Add the lemon juice and season with salt and pepper.

7. Add the Brussels sprouts and mix. Garnish with Parmesan and serve immediately.

Time-Saving Tip: You can purchase vegetable broth in the soup aisle. You can also find jars of vegetable broth paste, which is a flavorful alternative.

PER SERVING: Calories: 1632; Total fat: 57g; Total carbs: 240g; Fiber: 19g; Sugar: 71g; Protein: 49g; Sodium: 1,117mg

Butternut Squash and Cauliflower Mac and Cheese

DAIRY-FREE, VEGETARIAN

This recipe turns a dairy-filled classic on its head by replacing the cheese with a combination of butternut squash, cashews, and nutritional yeast.

Serves 4   **Prep time: 15 minutes / Cook time: 25 minutes**

1 butternut squash,
   peeled and cubed
½ head cauliflower florets
10 ounces pasta
½ cup raw cashews
½ cup vegetable broth
½ cup nutritional yeast
1 teaspoon
   yellow mustard
2 teaspoons olive oil

1. Boil 2 cups water in a large pot. Add the butternut squash and boil for 3 minutes, then add the cauliflower and cook for 4 minutes, or until the squash and cauliflower are soft and easily pierced by a fork. Drain.

2. In a separate pot, bring 2 cups water to a boil and cook the pasta according to the package directions. Drain.

3. Place the squash, cauliflower, cashews, vegetable broth, nutritional yeast, and yellow mustard into a blender. Blend on high speed until smooth.

4. Place the drained noodles and olive oil in a pot. Pour the butternut squash mixture over the noodles and stir until the noodles are saturated. Serve immediately.

Substitution Tip: You can replace the butternut squash with canned pumpkin puree.

PER SERVING: Calories: 596; Total fat: 14g; Total carbs: 93g; Fiber: 15g; Sugar: 7g; Protein: 31g; Sodium: 311mg

Herbed Garlic Cauliflower Mash

GLUTEN-FREE, ONE POT, VEGETARIAN

A nutritious alternative to mashed potatoes, cauliflower has a similar flavor and texture. This mash is perfect for holidays as well as casual dinners.

Serves 2   **Prep time: 15 minutes / Cook time: 25 minutes**

4 tablespoons olive oil
2 rosemary sprigs
5 garlic cloves, minced
2 large heads
   cauliflower, chopped
2 cups vegetable broth
2 tablespoons
   unsalted butter
½ cup unsweetened
   nondairy milk
Salt
Freshly ground
   black pepper

1. In a large pot, heat the olive oil over medium heat. Add the rosemary and garlic and cook for 4 minutes.

2. Add the cauliflower and cook for 6 minutes, or until it begins to soften.

3. Add the vegetable broth and bring to a boil. Cover, and reduce the heat to a simmer. Simmer for about 10 minutes.

4. Drain the cauliflower, reserving the liquid.

5. Transfer the cauliflower to a large bowl, and add the butter, milk, and ¼ cup of the cauliflower liquid. Mash thoroughly. Season with salt and pepper. Serve immediately.

Meal-Prep Tip: Make extra cauliflower mash for another easy recipe. Roll the mash into small balls and fry with 1 tablespoon olive oil over medium heat.

PER SERVING: Calories: 611; Total fat: 42g; Total carbs: 54g; Fiber: 23g; Sugar: 25g; Protein: 19g; Sodium: 896mg

Green Bean Casserole

DAIRY-FREE, VEGAN

This recipe elevates the traditional bean casserole with onions and mushrooms. Bring it to your next holiday party.

Serves 4   **Prep time: 15 minutes / Cook time: 35 minutes**

1 pound green beans,
  fresh or frozen
2 tablespoons olive oil
1 onion, chopped
8 ounces
  mushrooms, sliced
1 cup vegetable broth
½ (13.5 ounce) can
  coconut milk
2 teaspoons
  all-purpose flour
1 teaspoon
  nutritional yeast
Salt
Freshly ground
  black pepper
Crispy onions, for serving
  (optional)
Sliced almonds, for
  serving (optional)

1. Preheat the oven to 400°F.

2. Cut the ends off the green beans and rinse. Boil in a pot of water for 6 minutes, drain, and set aside.

3. In a medium skillet, heat the olive oil over medium heat. Add the onion and cook for 3 minutes, or until translucent.

4. Add the mushrooms and cook for 4 minutes. Add the vegetable broth, coconut milk, and flour. Mix until the sauce thickens. Add the nutritional yeast, and season with salt and pepper.

5. Add the cooked green beans to the pot and mix. Cook for another 5 minutes.

6. Transfer the mixture to a baking dish and bake, uncovered, for 15 minutes.

7. Serve with crispy onions or sliced almonds (if using). You can store leftovers in an airtight container in the refrigerator for up to 3 days.

Shopping Tip: Choose bright green beans that are firm to the touch.

PER SERVING: Calories: 187; Total fat: 14g; Total carbs: 16g; Fiber: 6g; Sugar: 4g; Protein: 6g; Sodium: 187mg

Butternut Squash Tacos

DAIRY-FREE, 5-INGREDIENT, GLUTEN-FREE, NUT-FREE, 30-MINUTE, VEGAN

Sweet and starchy butternut squash makes a great taco filling. This recipe goes well with Spicy Cashew Cheese (page 143).

Serves 2 **Prep time: 15 minutes / Cook time: 15 minutes**

1 butternut squash,
  halved and seeded
1 sweet potato, halved
1 (15-ounce) can black
  beans, drained
  and rinsed
Salt
1 lime, sliced
6 corn tortillas
Shredded cheese of
  choice, for serving
  (optional)

1. Preheat the oven to 400°F.
2. Place the butternut squash and sweet potato in the oven and roast for 15 minutes, or until soft.
3. In a small pan, heat the black beans. Season with salt and lime.
4. Scoop a small amount of black beans onto each tortilla.
5. Scoop out the flesh from the butternut squash and place into the tortillas. Repeat with the sweet potato.
6. Top with cheese (if using) and serve immediately.

Time-Saving Tip: You can find peeled and chopped butternut squash in the produce section of the grocery store.

PER SERVING: Calories: 541; Total fat: 3g; Total carbs: 117g; Fiber: 25g; Sugar: 11g; Protein: 20g; Sodium: 161mg

Double-Stuffed Baked Potato

5-INGREDIENT, GLUTEN-FREE, NUT-FREE, ONE POT, VEGAN

This double-stuffed baked potato with kale packs a vitamin punch. You can add any leafy greens you have in your refrigerator.

Serves 4   **Prep time: 5 minutes / Cook time: 40 minutes**

4 russet potatoes
2 cups whole or
** nondairy milk**
2 cups kale, chopped
Salt
Freshly ground
** black pepper**

1. Preheat the oven to 425°F.
2. Place the potatoes in the oven and bake for 30 minutes, or until soft.
3. Scoop out the potato flesh and place in a bowl.
4. Add the milk and kale. Season with salt and pepper.
5. Spoon the filling into the potato skins and continue baking for another 10 minutes.
6. Serve immediately with your topping of choice. Some great options are barbecue sauce, cheese, vegan mayonnaise, salsa, guacamole, caramelized onions, ketchup, or hot sauce.

Meal-Prep Tip: Throw some extra potatoes in the oven to have on hand. You can store them, wrapped in aluminum foil, in the refrigerator for up to 3 days. Chop the baked potatoes to serve in omelets or curries, or even fry them up for breakfast.

PER SERVING: Calories: 237; Total fat: 4g; Total carbs: 43g; Fiber: 6g; Sugar: 9g; Protein: 9g; Sodium: 115mg

Autumn Harvest Medley

DAIRY-FREE, GLUTEN-FREE, VEGAN

This harvest medley, served over potatoes instead of the usual rice, is a great way to use up your fall produce. The apple adds sweetness and crunch.

Serves 2   **Prep time: 15 minutes / Cook time: 20 minutes**

8 ounces broccoli florets

8 ounces cauliflower florets

1 sweet potato, peeled and chopped

1 apple, cubed

2 beets, cubed

3 tablespoons olive oil

1 teaspoon onion powder

1 teaspoon ground cinnamon

Salt

Freshly ground black pepper

5 potatoes, cubed

¼ cup nondairy milk

1 lemon, sliced

1. Preheat the oven to 400°F.

2. Place the broccoli, cauliflower, sweet potato, apple, and beets on a large baking sheet and drizzle with olive oil. Sprinkle with the onion powder and cinnamon. Season with salt and pepper.

3. Bake for 20 minutes, or until the vegetables are tender.

4. In a separate pot, bring 3 cups water to a boil. Add the potatoes and cook for 10 minutes, until soft.

5. Drain the potatoes and transfer to a large bowl.

6. Add the nondairy milk and mash to your desired consistency. Season with salt and pepper.

7. Divide the mashed potatoes between two plates. Top with the roasted vegetables. Season with lemon, salt, and pepper.

Prep Tip: When cubing the apple, be sure to remove and discard the seeded core.

PER SERVING: Calories: 774; Total fat: 23g; Total carbs: 134g; Fiber: 26g; Sugar: 33g; Protein: 18g; Sodium: 228mg

■ ROASTED BEET COCONUT CREAM CHOWDER
PAGE 109

5

chapter five winter
December Through February

Winter is the season for avocado, winter squash, sweet potatoes, Brussels sprouts, celery, collard greens, and potatoes.

Root Veggie Soup with Barley

DAIRY-FREE, VEGAN

Blended coconut milk and cashews make this soup creamy and satisfying. Nutrient-rich barley absorbs the flavor of the other ingredients.

Serves 2 **Prep time: 10 minutes / Cook time: 30 minutes**

½ cup barley
2 teaspoons olive oil
1 shallot, diced
3 cups vegetable broth
3 Yukon Gold
  potatoes, chopped
2 beets
½ (13.5-ounce) can
  coconut cream
¼ cup raw cashews
Pinch salt
Pinch freshly ground
  black pepper
Fresh parsley, for garnish
  (optional)

1. Bring 2 cups water to a boil. Add the barley and cover. Reduce the heat to a simmer and cook for 25 minutes, or until the barley is tender. Set aside.

2. In a medium pot, heat the olive oil over medium heat. Add the shallot and cook for 4 minutes. Add the vegetable broth and bring to a boil.

3. Add the potatoes and beets, and bring back to a boil. Reduce the heat to a simmer, cover, and cook for 15 minutes.

4. While the soup boils, put the coconut cream and cashews in a blender. Blend on high speed until smooth.

5. Pour the mixture into the soup, and stir to combine. Season with salt and pepper to taste.

6. Add the cooked barley and stir.

7. Check the beets and potatoes with a fork. If they are soft, turn off the heat and set aside. If either is still firm, cook for 5 minutes more, or until desired consistency. Garnish with parsley (if using) and serve warm.

Meal-Prep Tip: Make extra barley to save for other meals. You can make 2 cups barley with 4 cups water.

PER SERVING: Calories: 950; Total fat: 30g; Total carbs: 160g; Fiber: 20g; Sugar: 69g; Protein: 17g; Sodium: 1,014mg

Roasted Beet Coconut Cream Chowder

GLUTEN-FREE

This beet chowder combines beets, parsnips, and sweet potatoes to create a hearty and beautifully colored soup. Pump up the protein by adding chickpeas or a garnish of toasted nuts.

Serves 4   **Prep time: 10 minutes / Cook time: 30 minutes**

2 tablespoons olive oil
1 onion, diced
5 beets, peeled and diced
1 parsnip, diced
1 sweet potato, peeled
  and diced
4 cups chicken broth
½ (13.5-ounce) can
  coconut cream
½ teaspoon ground sage
Pinch salt
Pinch freshly ground
  black pepper
Plain Greek yogurt,
  for serving
2 teaspoons sunflower
  seeds, for serving

1. In a large pot, heat the olive oil over medium heat. Add the onion and cook for 4 minutes.

2. Add the beets, parsnip, and sweet potato and cook for 5 minutes.

3. Add the chicken broth. Bring to a boil, cover, and simmer for 25 minutes.

4. Add the coconut cream and cook for 3 minutes, stirring frequently.

5. Season with sage, salt, and pepper.

6. Pour into a blender and blend until smooth. Work in batches if needed.

7. Divide the soup among 4 bowls and serve with a dollop of yogurt in the center. Garnish with sunflower seeds.

Time-Saving Tip: Purchase peeled beets.

PER SERVING: Calories: 438; Total fat: 18g; Total carbs: 59g; Fiber: 6g; Sugar: 44g; Protein: 12g; Sodium: 753mg

Split Pea Soup

Split pea soup is usually made with bacon or ham, but this version gets its umami flavor from vegetable broth and soy sauce. Leeks, celery, and peas provide vitamins.

Serves 4   **Prep time: 5 minutes / Cook time: 20 minutes**

2 tablespoons olive oil

1 onion, diced

2 leeks, tough layer removed, rinsed well, and finely sliced

2 celery, diced

2 (10- to 12-ounce) bags frozen peas

7 cups vegetable broth

1 teaspoon soy sauce

Salt

Freshly ground black pepper

¾ cup Greek yogurt

1. In a large pot, heat the olive oil over medium heat.
2. Add the onion and leeks and cook for 4 minutes.
3. Add the celery and cook for 3 minutes, stirring occasionally.
4. Add the peas and vegetable broth and bring to a boil. Reduce the heat to a simmer and cook for 10 minutes.
5. Transfer 1 cup of the mixture to the blender. Blend on high speed until smooth. Pour the blended soup back into the pot.
6. Season with salt and pepper.
7. Serve with a dollop of yogurt.

Prep Tip: For a smoky flavor, add smoked paprika or liquid smoke.

PER SERVING: Calories: 452; Total fat: 8g; Total carbs: 67g; Fiber: 20g; Sugar: 25g; Protein: 26g; Sodium: 1,422mg

Sweet Potato Soup

DAIRY-FREE, GLUTEN-FREE, 30-MINUTE, VEGAN

This hearty vegetable potato soup with kale and carrots is comfort food for a rainy day. Avocado provides healthy fat, which is good for cellular function and brain health. The soup is made with fresh, whole food ingredients and packed with tons of healthy vitamins and minerals.

Serves 4   Prep time: 10 minutes / Cook time: 20 minutes

2 tablespoons olive oil
1 large onion, chopped
1 large carrot, chopped
2 sweet potatoes, chopped
2 cups vegetable stock, plus more as needed
¾ cup nondairy milk
1 tablespoon nutritional yeast
2 tablespoons tomato paste
2 cups stemmed chopped kale
2 cups sweet corn
½ avocado, diced (optional)

1. In a medium pot, heat the olive oil over medium heat. Cook the onion and carrot for 3 minutes, until they start to soften.

2. Add the potatoes, vegetable stock, milk, and nutritional yeast.

3. Simmer over medium heat, covered, for 20 minutes, or until the potatoes soften. If the soup is too thick, you can add more vegetable stock.

4. Add the kale and corn, and cook for an additional 3 minutes, or until the kale has wilted.

5. Serve immediately with the avocado (if using), or store in an airtight container in the refrigerator for up to 3 days.

Time-Saving Tip: You can buy pre-washed and chopped kale to make this recipe even easier.

PER SERVING: Calories: 217; Total fat: 2g; Total carbs: 45g; Fiber: 8g; Sugar: 12g; Protein: 9g; Sodium: 178mg

Spaghetti Squash with Kale

5-INGREDIENT, GLUTEN-FREE, NUT-FREE

Spaghetti squash is low carb, gluten free, and nutrient rich. When you roast a spaghetti squash and cut it in half, you'll find out why the name is so fitting. You can use a fork to shred the squash to create strand-like noodles to serve with your favorite pasta sauce, or even simply a little olive oil, salt, and pepper.

Serves 3   **Prep time: 5 minutes / Cook time: 35 minutes**

1 spaghetti squash
4 tablespoons olive oil, divided
2 tablespoons butter
12 ounces shrimp
Juice of 1 lemon
Salt
Freshly ground black pepper
5 kale leaves, chopped

1. Preheat the oven to 400°F.
2. Slice the spaghetti squash in half, lengthwise, and scoop out the seeds.
3. Drizzle the inside of the spaghetti squash with 2 tablespoons of olive oil.
4. Place the spaghetti squash facedown on a large baking sheet. Bake for 35 minutes, or until the squash begins to brown slightly and the inside comes apart easily with a fork.
5. While the squash cooks, melt the butter in a large skillet over medium heat. Add the shrimp and cook, stirring occasionally, until they turn pink.
6. Drizzle the shrimp with the lemon juice and set aside.

7. Use a fork to shred the insides of the squash and create strands. Transfer the strands to a separate bowl.

8. Season the strands with the remaining 2 tablespoons of olive oil, salt, pepper, and mix in the chopped kale. The heat will wilt the kale.

9. Add the shrimp and mix until the squash is coated with olive oil. Serve immediately.

Time-Saving Tip: A smaller spaghetti squash will take less time in the oven, so choose one that's on the smaller side.

PER SERVING: Calories: 407; Total fat: 29g; Total carbs: 14g; Fiber: 0g; Sugar: 0g; Protein: 26g; Sodium: 350mg

Roasted Brussels Sprouts, Sausage, and Creamy Gnocchi

DAIRY-FREE, 30-MINUTE

This recipe takes less than 30 minutes to make and makes a great dinner after a long day. The roasted Brussels sprouts add crunch, and the sausage pairs perfectly with the cream sauce. To make this meal vegan, omit the sausage or use a vegan sausage.

Serves 2   **Prep time: 5 minutes / Cook time: 25 minutes**

2 (12-ounce) boxes gnocchi

2 tablespoons olive oil

8 ounces Brussels sprouts, halved

½ teaspoon freshly ground black pepper

2 sausages, halved and sliced

⅓ cup vegetable broth

¼ cup coconut cream

3 teaspoons nutritional yeast

2 teaspoons soy sauce

3 large collard leaves

1. Bring 3 cups water to a boil. Add the gnocchi, and reduce the heat to low. Cook for 5 to 6 minutes, or until the gnocchi float to the top. Drain and set aside.

2. In a wok, heat the olive oil over medium heat.

3. Add the Brussels sprouts and pepper, and cook for 4 minutes, stirring frequently.

4. Add the sausage and cook for 5 minutes.

5. Add the vegetable broth, coconut cream, nutritional yeast, and soy sauce. Stir together.

6. Add the gnocchi and continue mixing until the sauce is absorbed.

7. Add the collard greens and continue mixing for 3 minutes, until the leaves are wilted. Serve with a crack of black pepper.

Time-Saving Tip: Purchase prechopped and halved Brussels sprouts.

PER SERVING: Calories: 1088; Total fat: 32g; Total carbs: 193g; Fiber: 20g; Sugar: 4g; Protein: 29g; Sodium: 3,123mg

Vegan Potato Salad

GLUTEN-FREE, VEGAN

This savory, sweet, and slightly sour potato salad is made crunchy by pickles and celery and tastes wonderful on its own, but you can also serve it topped with cheese in a sandwich.

Serves 4   **Prep time: 10 minutes / Cook time: 30 minutes**

7 russet potatoes, peeled and diced

1 tablespoon salt, plus more for seasoning

1½ cups vegan mayonnaise

2 tablespoons apple cider vinegar

1 tablespoon yellow mustard

½ cup sliced celery

2 dill pickles, diced

Juice of 1 lemon

¼ teaspoon freshly ground black pepper

1. Place the potatoes and 1 tablespoon of salt in a large pot and add enough water to cover the potatoes.

2. Bring the water to a boil, cover, and reduce the heat to maintain a simmer. Cook for 25 minutes. Drain the potatoes in a large colander and let cool for 5 minutes.

3. In a bowl, mix the mayonnaise, vinegar, mustard, celery, and pickles.

4. When the potatoes are cool enough to handle, chop them into quarters and place them in a bowl. Add the creamy mixture and mix until evenly distributed.

5. Season with lemon juice, salt, pepper, or even a splash of pickle juice!

6. Serve warm or set in the refrigerator to cool before serving.

Meal-Prep Tip: When you boil the potatoes, make extra and store them in an airtight container in the refrigerator for up to 2 days. They are great to have on hand for making breakfast potatoes, omelets, or soup.

PER SERVING: Calories: 477; Total fat: 22g; Total carbs: 66g; Fiber: 10g; Sugar: 5g; Protein: 7g; Sodium: 1,411mg

Ramen with Bok Choy and Sesame Oil

DAIRY-FREE, NUT-FREE, 30-MINUTE

This ramen is loaded with bok choy, a cruciferous vegetable that boosts the immune system.

Serves 4   **Prep time: 5 minutes / Cook time: 25 minutes**

2 teaspoons olive oil

1 teaspoon peeled fresh ginger, minced

3 garlic cloves, minced

2 teaspoons soy sauce

4 cups chicken broth

½ jalapeño, sliced

2 eggs

3 ounces dried ramen noodles

2 bunches bok choy

2 teaspoons sesame oil

1. In a pot, heat the olive oil over medium heat. Add the ginger and garlic and cook for 4 minutes, stirring frequently.

2. Add the soy sauce and chicken broth and bring to a boil. Add the jalapeño and reduce the heat to a simmer.

3. In a separate small pot, bring 2 cups water to a boil. Add the eggs. Cover and cook for 6 minutes.

4. While the eggs boil, prepare a bowl of ice water. Ladle the eggs into the ice water to cool.

5. Do not turn off the heat under the small pot. Add the ramen noodles. Cook per the package instructions.

6. Add the bok choy to the simmering vegetable broth and cook for 2 minutes. Turn off the heat and remove from the stove.

7. Assemble the cooked ramen in 4 large bowls. Pour the broth with the bok choy over the noodles.

8. Peel the eggs, slice them in half, place one half on top of the noodles.

9. Drizzle with sesame oil and serve immediately.

Meal-Prep Tip: Assemble the soup in a large mason jar and store in the refrigerator overnight for a delicious and portable lunch.

PER SERVING: Calories: 168; Total fat: 10g; Total carbs: 10g; Fiber: 1g; Sugar: 1g; Protein: 9g; Sodium: 1,004mg

Vegetable Stew with Drop Dumplings

DAIRY-FREE, NUT-FREE, 30-MINUTE, VEGAN

In this recipe, vegetable stew gets a twist: Drop dumplings replace noodles. The dumplings require minimal effort and cook right in the broth.

Serves 4   **Prep time: 5 minutes / Cook time: 25 minutes**

4 cups vegetable broth
3 potatoes, cubed
2 small carrots, chopped
2 celery stalks, chopped
1 cup all-purpose flour
4 teaspoons
   baking powder
1 teaspoon salt
Freshly ground
   black pepper
1 lemon, sliced

1. Pour the vegetable broth into a large pot and bring to a boil. Add the potatoes and cook for 3 minutes.

2. Add the carrots, cover, reduce the heat to medium, and cook for 10 minutes.

3. Add the celery, cover, and simmer.

4. In a bowl, mix the flour, baking powder, and salt.

5. Add ½ cup of water and mix until a dough is formed.

6. Remove the lid from the soup and increase the heat. When the broth is boiling, drop spoonfuls of dough into the broth. Continue until all the dough is gone.

7. Cover, reduce the heat, and simmer for 7 minutes. Adjust the seasoning and add lemon slices. Serve immediately.

Shopping Tip: Vegetable broth is usually sold in a carton. Buy a few at a time and keep them in your pantry.

Substitution Tip: Use gluten-free flour to make this stew gluten free.

PER SERVING: Calories: 271; Total fat: 1g; Total carbs: 59g; Fiber: 7g; Sugar: 7g; Protein: 7g; Sodium: 1,164mg

Sweet Potato and Black Bean Chili

GLUTEN-FREE, NUT-FREE, VEGETARIAN

This chili delivers sweetness with a bit of spice. A dollop of Greek yogurt and slices of avocado balance the heat.

Serves 4   **Prep time: 10 minutes / Cook time: 31 minutes**

2 cups vegetable broth, divided

1 onion, chopped

2 carrots, chopped

2 sweet potatoes, chopped

3 garlic cloves

2 tomatoes, diced

2 tablespoons ground cumin

2 (15-ounce) cans black beans, drained and rinsed

1 avocado, diced (optional)

Greek yogurt, for serving (optional)

Tortilla chips, for serving (optional)

1. In a large pot over medium heat, heat ¼ cup of vegetable broth. Add the onion, carrots, sweet potatoes, and garlic and cook for 6 minutes.

2. Add the tomatoes and cumin. Cook for 5 minutes.

3. Stir in the black beans and remaining 1¾ cups of vegetable broth.

4. Cook, uncovered, for 20 minutes.

5. Scoop out 1 cup of the soup and blend until smooth. Pour the blended cup of soup back into the pot and stir.

6. Divide the soup evenly among 4 bowls. Serve with avocado, a dollop of yogurt, or tortilla chips (if using).

Time-Saving Tip: If you have a slow cooker, cook all the ingredients for 8 hours on low. By dinnertime, you'll have a delicious meal ready to eat.

PER SERVING: Calories: 283; Total fat: 2g; Total carbs: 55g; Fiber: 16g; Sugar: 8g; Protein: 14g; Sodium: 333mg

Baked Potato Soup

GLUTEN-FREE, VEGAN

Nutritional yeast adds a cheese flavor to this unbelievably creamy soup. Try serving it in a bread bowl.

Serves 6   **Prep time: 5 minutes / Cook time: 30 minutes**

1 tablespoon olive oil
1 yellow onion, diced
5 medium russet potatoes, diced
Salt
Freshly ground black pepper
4 cups vegetable broth
3 tablespoons nutritional yeast
½ cup coconut cream
½ cup raw cashews, soaked overnight, drained

1. In a large pot, heat the olive oil over medium heat.
2. Add the onion and cook for 4 minutes, or until translucent.
3. Add the potatoes and stir. Season with salt and pepper and cook for 6 minutes, stirring frequently.
4. Add the vegetable broth and nutritional yeast and bring to a boil. Once boiling, cover, reduce the heat to low, and simmer for 15 minutes.
5. Add the coconut cream and cashews to the blender. Blend on high speed until smooth. Set aside.
6. Remove the soup from the heat and pour the coconut-cashew mixture into the soup.
7. Transfer the soup into the blender, working in batches as needed, and blend, until smooth.
8. Ladle the soup into bowls and serve immediately.

Time-Saving Tip: Instead of soaking your cashews overnight, you can boil them for 15 minutes.

PER SERVING: Calories: 280; Total fat: 7g; Total carbs: 49g; Fiber: 7g; Sugar: 17g; Protein: 8g; Sodium: 403mg

Curry-Stuffed Japanese Sweet Potato

DAIRY-FREE, GLUTEN-FREE, VEGAN

This recipe calls for Japanese sweet potatoes, which are relatively starchy and sweet, but you can use any type. Adjust the spice level to your liking, and try adding a cooling garnish like Greek yogurt or sour cream.

Serves 4 **Prep time: 5 minutes / Cook time: 45 minutes**

3 small Japanese sweet potatoes

2 tablespoons olive oil

1-inch piece fresh ginger, peeled and grated

3 garlic cloves, minced

1 tablespoon red curry paste, plus more as needed

½ cup coconut cream, plus more for serving

1 (15-ounce) can chickpeas, drained and rinsed

1. Preheat the oven to 425°F. Line a baking sheet with parchment paper.

2. Pierce the skin of the sweet potatoes several times with a fork, put the sweet potatoes on the prepared sheet, and place in the oven for 45 minutes.

3. In a medium skillet, heat the olive oil over medium heat. Add the ginger and garlic and cook for 4 minutes, stirring frequently.

4. Stir in the red curry paste. Add the coconut cream and taste. Add more curry paste as needed according to your taste. Cook for 5 minutes.

5. Stir in the chickpeas until they are saturated. Continue cooking for 7 minutes. Reduce the heat to a simmer.

6. When the sweet potatoes are done, you should be able to easily pierce them with a fork. Remove them from the oven and let cool until they are safe to touch.

7. Cut the sweet potatoes lengthwise down the center.

8. Scoop a generous amount of the curry into the center of each sweet potato.

9. Top with a dollop of coconut cream and serve immediately.

Meal-Prep Tip: Bake several sweet potatoes at a time. You can store them in an airtight container in the refrigerator for up to 3 days. Remake this recipe or use them in other delicious dishes, such as soups or stir-fries.

PER SERVING: Calories: 340; Total fat: 9g; Total carbs: 59g; Fiber: 5g; Sugar: 23g; Protein: 8g; Sodium: 213mg

Stuffed Delicata Squash

DAIRY-FREE, GLUTEN-FREE, NUT-FREE, VEGAN

Less robust than other squash, the delicata is small and its thin skin is edible, making prep easy. You can garnish it with nuts and Spicy Cashew Cheese (page 143).

Serves 3   **Prep time: 5 minutes / Cook time: 35 minutes**

2 delicata squash, halved and seeded
1 tablespoon maple syrup
1 teaspoon ground cinnamon, divided
Salt
Freshly ground black pepper
2 tablespoons olive oil
2 shallots, thinly sliced
1 apple, cored and diced
1 (14-ounce) block firm tofu
1 teaspoon all-purpose seasoning powder
3 large collard green leaves, chopped

1. Preheat the oven to 400°F.
2. Place the squash halves faceup on a baking sheet. Brush the maple syrup on the insides and sprinkle with ½ teaspoon of cinnamon. Season with salt and pepper. Place in the oven for 25 to 30 minutes.
3. In a large skillet, heat the olive oil over medium heat. Add the shallots and cook for 4 minutes, stirring frequently.
4. Add the apple and cook for 4 minutes.
5. With your hands, crumble the tofu onto the skillet. Add the remaining ½ teaspoon of cinnamon and the seasoning powder. Season with salt and pepper. Cook for 5 minutes, stirring frequently.
6. Add the collard green leaves and stir. Cook for 3 minutes, then turn off the heat and continue mixing. The heat will naturally wilt the leaves.
7. Remove the squash from the oven and wait until it is cool enough to handle.
8. Scoop generous amounts of the tofu mixture into the squash. Place the squash back in the oven and cook for 5 minutes. Serve immediately.

Meal-Prep Tip: Make extra tofu stuffing and store in an airtight container in the refrigerator up to 4 days. It's delicious in tacos and burritos.

PER SERVING: Calories: 286; Total fat: 14g; Total carbs: 19g; Fiber: 6g; Sugar: 19g; Protein: 12g; Sodium: 69mg

Root Vegetable Mash with Salmon

The blend of sweet and savory veggies in this mash pairs perfectly with salmon.

Serves 2   **Prep time: 5 minutes / Cook time: 40 minutes**

2 parsnips, peeled
  and diced
1 sweet potato, peeled
  and diced
2 potatoes, diced
1 rutabaga, diced
2 salmon fillets
Salt
Freshly ground
  black pepper
1 teaspoon butter
2 teaspoons unsweetened
  nondairy milk
1 teaspoon dried
  rosemary
3 garlic cloves, minced
1 lemon

1. Preheat the oven to 400°F.

2. Bring a large pot of water to a boil. Add the parsnips and cook for 10 minutes.

3. Add the sweet potato, potatoes, and rutabaga. Bring back to a boil, cover, and reduce the heat to a simmer. Cook for 20 minutes, or until the vegetables are soft.

4. Place the salmon in a baking dish. Season with salt and pepper.

5. Bake the salmon for 15 minutes, or until it flakes easily with a fork.

6. Drain the vegetables in a large colander and transfer to a large bowl.

7. Add the butter, milk, rosemary, and garlic. Season with salt and pepper.

8. Mash with a potato masher until you reach your desired consistency.

CONTINUED

9. Serve warm with the salmon. Season with pepper and the juice of ½ lemon.

10. Store leftover mash in an airtight container in the freezer for up to 2 weeks.

Prep Tip: The time in the oven will vary depending on the thickness and size of the salmon fillets. Check the salmon after 10 minutes to see if it has a flaky consistency. If not, continue baking up to 6 minutes, checking every 3 minutes.

PER SERVING: Calories: 614; Total fat: 19g; Total carbs: 89g; Fiber: 19g; Sugar: 24g; Protein: 28g; Sodium: 150mg

Chickpea Lasagna Soup

DAIRY-FREE, NUT-FREE, ONE POT, VEGAN

This soup is reminiscent of a classic chicken noodle soup—with a vegan twist. Packed with protein from the chickpeas and a touch of cheesy flavor from the nutritional yeast, it is sure to please on any cold winter night.

Serves 5   **Prep time: 10 minutes / Cook time: 30 minutes**

2 tablespoons olive oil

1 yellow onion,
   chopped fine

3 carrots, cut into
   ¼-inch-thick slices

2 celery stalks, cut into
   ¼-inch-thick slices

Salt

Freshly ground
   black pepper

4 tablespoons
   nutritional yeast

6 cups vegetable broth

2 (15-ounce) cans
   chickpeas, drained
   and rinsed

1 box lasagna noodles

1. In a large pot, heat the olive oil over medium heat. Add the onion, carrots, and celery. Season with salt and pepper and cook for 5 minutes, stirring occasionally.

2. Add the nutritional yeast and cook for 2 minutes, stirring occasionally.

3. Slowly pour in the broth, and then add the chickpeas.

4. Bring the broth to a boil, cover, and reduce the heat to maintain a simmer. Continue cooking, covered, for 5 minutes.

5. Add the lasagna noodles to the pot, cover, and bring back to a boil. Once boiling, reduce the heat to a simmer and cook for 10 minutes, covered. The noodles should be tender.

6. Season with salt and pepper. Serve immediately.

Time-Saving Tip: Slice the celery and carrots at the same time for equal-size pieces.

PER SERVING: Calories: 596; Total fat: 6g; Total carbs: 108g; Fiber: 16g; Sugar: 12g; Protein: 29g; Sodium: 720mg

Cauliflower Crust Veggie Pizza

GLUTEN-FREE, NUT-FREE, VEGETARIAN

An antioxidant-rich cauliflower crust makes this a delicious and healthy alternative to traditional pizza. Topped with cheese and greens, it's packed with plenty of nutrients.

Serves 4   **Prep time: 10 minutes / Cook time: 30 minutes**

3 cups cauliflower rice, frozen or fresh

1 egg

1 cup shredded Parmesan cheese, plus more for topping

½ teaspoon garlic powder

1 tablespoon olive oil

½ cup pizza sauce

Shredded mozzarella cheese or vegan cheese

½ cup arugula

½ cup spinach

½ cup sliced mushrooms

1. Preheat the oven to 425°F.

2. Line a baking sheet with parchment paper and spread the cauliflower rice in a single layer on the prepared sheet. Bake for 5 minutes.

3. In a large bowl, place the baked cauliflower rice, egg, Parmesan, and garlic powder. Mix to combine into a dough.

4. Line the same baking sheet with parchment paper and place the dough on top. Place another piece of parchment paper on top of the dough.

5. Using your hands or a rolling pin, roll the dough to form a round crust ¼ to ½ inch thick with a raised wall around the edges.

6. Remove the top layer of parchment paper and bake for 15 minutes. Remove the pizza crust and top with olive oil.

7. Spread the pizza sauce evenly onto the crust. Top with the cheese.

8. Add the arugula, spinach, and mushrooms and put the pizza back in the oven. Bake for 10 minutes.

CONTINUED

9. Remove from the oven, top with Parmesan cheese, and serve hot. You can store leftovers in an airtight container for up to 3 days.

Substitution Tip: To make the dough vegan, substitute the egg for a flax egg (1 tablespoon ground flaxseed meal mixed with 3 tablespoons water) and omit the Parmesan cheese.

PER SERVING: Calories: 221; Total fat: 14g; Total carbs: 10g; Fiber: 3g; Sugar: 3g; Protein: 16g; Sodium: 508mg

Pumpkin Curry Bowl

DAIRY-FREE, ONE POT, VEGAN

This bowl's fragrant curry paste and sweet pumpkin puree are a winter dream team. Coconut cream makes the curry sweet; adjust it to your preferred level of spiciness.

Serves 4   **Prep time: 10 minutes / Cook time: 30 minutes**

1 tablespoon olive oil
1 small onion, diced
3 tablespoons curry paste
½ (15-ounce) can
  pumpkin puree
¼ cup vegetable broth
2 carrots, thinly sliced
2 sweet potatoes, peeled
  and diced
⅓ cup coconut cream,
  plus more as needed

1. In a large skillet, heat the olive oil over medium heat. Add the onion and cook for 4 minutes, or until translucent.

2. Add the curry paste and stir. Cook for 2 minutes.

3. Pour in the pumpkin puree and mix the ingredients well. Add the vegetable broth and cook for 5 minutes.

4. Add the carrots and sweet potatoes, and bring the liquid to a boil. Reduce to a simmer, cover, and cook for 15 minutes.

5. Stir in the coconut cream and taste. If the curry is too spicy, add more coconut cream.

6. Serve alone, or pair it with Mango Chutney (page 146) and brown or white rice.

Shopping Tip: Curry paste is sold at most grocery stores in the international food aisle with the Asian and Indian products. If you can't find it, curry powder works great, too.

PER SERVING: Calories: 220; Total fat: 12g; Total carbs: 27g; Fiber: 5g; Sugar: 8g; Protein: 4g; Sodium: 111mg

Nourishing Winter Quiche

5-INGREDIENT, GLUTEN-FREE, NUT-FREE, ONE POT, VEGETARIAN

Make this quiche creamy by whisking the eggs and nondairy milk. This recipe uses potatoes and sweet potatoes, but you can use any produce you have on hand.

Serves 4   **Prep time: 10 minutes / Cook time: 25 minutes**

2 tablespoons olive oil, plus more as needed
½ onion, chopped
2 potatoes, peeled and diced
1 sweet potato, peeled and diced
5 eggs
½ cup milk or nondairy milk
Pinch salt
Pinch freshly ground black pepper

1. Preheat the oven to 400°F.
2. In a cast-iron skillet, heat the olive oil over medium heat. Add the onion and cook for 2 minutes, or until translucent.
3. Add the potatoes and sweet potato and more olive oil, if needed. Cook for 5 minutes. Reduce the heat to low, cover, and cook for 5 minutes.
4. In a large bowl, whisk together the eggs, milk, salt, and pepper until blended.
5. Pour the egg mixture over the potatoes.
6. Put the cast-iron skillet in the oven, covered with an oven-safe lid or foil, and bake for 15 minutes.
7. Remove the cast-iron skillet from the oven, and let cool. Serve with a crack of black pepper.

Substitution Tip: Replace the eggs with tofu and use nondairy milk to make this dish vegan.

PER SERVING: Calories: 261; Total fat: 13g; Total carbs: 27g; Fiber: 4g; Sugar: 5g; Protein: 10g; Sodium: 155mg

Cauliflower Grilled Cheese

GLUTEN-FREE, NUT-FREE, 30-MINUTE, VEGETARIAN

This herbed cauliflower crust melts in your mouth, along with the cheese. Pair it with your favorite soup.

Serves 4 **Prep time: 10 minutes / Cook time: 20 minutes**

2 tablespoon olive oil, divided

2 teaspoons dried rosemary

2 onions, diced

1 teaspoon brown sugar

1 (16-ounce) bag cauliflower florets

2 eggs

½ cup finely grated Parmesan cheese

1 teaspoon dried oregano

Salt

Freshly ground black pepper

1 cup shredded Gruyère or Cheddar cheese

1. In a medium skillet, heat 1 tablespoon of olive oil over medium-low heat. Add the rosemary and onions, and cook for 4 minutes.

2. Sprinkle the brown sugar over the onions and cook, stirring frequently, for 3 minutes. Set the onions aside.

3. Put the cauliflower florets in the food processor and process until the mixture resembles cauliflower rice.

4. Put the eggs, Parmesan cheese, and oregano in the food processor and pulse until the ingredients are mixed well. Season with salt and pepper.

5. Heat a large skillet over medium heat and add the remaining 1 tablespoon of olive oil.

6. Form a small patty of the cauliflower mixture and place in the skillet. Use a fork or spatula to flatten it.

7. Cook for 5 minutes, or until golden and crispy. Flip and cook another 5 minutes. Repeat with the rest of the cauliflower mixture.

CONTINUED

8. Top one of the cauliflower slices with cheese and place the other cauliflower slice on top. Cook until the cheese is melted, about 2 minutes. Transfer to a plate and serve immediately.

Substitution Tip: To make this dairy free, use Spicy Cashew Cheese (page 143) or vegan cheese.

PER SERVING: Calories: 325; Total fat: 22g; Total carbs: 18g; Fiber: 6g; Sugar: 8g; Protein: 19g; Sodium: 434mg

Cauliflower "Meatball" Whole-Wheat Pasta

DAIRY-FREE, NUT-FREE, VEGAN

These vitamin- and mineral-rich cauliflower meatballs will be a hit even among your meat-eating friends.

Serves 2   **Prep time: 10 minutes / Cook time: 35 minutes**

½ **head cauliflower florets**
2 **tablespoons olive oil, divided**
½ **yellow onion, minced finely**
2 **garlic cloves, minced**
1 **cup oats**
½ **cup bread crumbs**
2 **teaspoons dried oregano**
Pinch salt
Pinch freshly ground black pepper
Cooked noodles, for serving

1. In a large pot, bring 3 cups water to a boil. Add the cauliflower. Bring back to a boil, and then reduce the heat to maintain a simmer and cook for 8 minutes, or until the cauliflower is soft. Drain the cauliflower in a colander.

2. In a medium pan, heat 1 tablespoon of olive oil over medium heat. Add the onion and garlic and cook for 3 minutes. Set aside.

3. Add the onion-garlic mix to a food processor with the cauliflower, oats, bread crumbs, oregano, salt, and pepper.

4. Blend until the ingredients are mixed together evenly.

5. Scoop out the mixture and form golf ball–size balls. Set aside.

6. In a nonstick pan, heat the remaining 1 tablespoon of olive oil over medium heat. Fry the cauliflower balls for 7 to 8 minutes, or until golden brown.

7. Serve immediately with noodles.

Shopping Tip: Buy prepackaged cauliflower florets.

PER SERVING: Calories: 401; Total fat: 18g; Total carbs: 52g; Fiber: 8g; Sugar: 5g; Protein: 10; Sodium: 189mg

Cauliflower Cream Fettuccine

DAIRY-FREE, 30-MINUTE, VEGAN

This fettuccine Alfredo tastes just like the real thing but is much higher in nutrients thanks to nutritional yeast, which is packed with B vitamins.

Serves 2   **Prep time: 5 minutes / Cook time: 25 minutes**

1 (16-ounce) package
    fettuccine noodles
1 tablespoon olive oil
1 onion, chopped
1 (16-ounce) bag
    cauliflower florets
2 tablespoons
    nutritional yeast
1 tablespoon soy sauce
½ (13.5-ounce) can
    coconut cream
Salt
Freshly ground
    black pepper
1 bunch fresh
    parsley, chopped

1. In a pot, bring 4 cups water to a boil. Add the fettuccine noodles. Lower the heat to simmer and cook for 10 minutes, or until the noodles are soft.

2. In a large pot, heat the olive oil over medium heat. Add the onion and cook for 4 minutes, or until translucent.

3. Add 4 cups water and bring to a boil. Add the cauliflower florets. Bring the liquid back to a boil, and then reduce the heat to maintain a simmer. Simmer the cauliflower for 10 minutes, or until soft.

4. Drain the cauliflower and transfer to a blender, along with the nutritional yeast, soy sauce, and coconut cream.

5. Blend on high speed, until the consistency is smooth. Season with salt and pepper.

6. Drain the fettuccine noodles and put them in the large pot. Pour the cauliflower cheese over the noodles and mix together.

7. Garnish with parsley and a crack of black pepper.

Shopping Tip: Buy prepacked cauliflower florets to save you some prep time.

Prep Tip: The key to making this recipe as cheesy as possible is to wait until the cauliflower has boiled to the point where it is falling apart.

PER SERVING: Calories: 1,447; Total fat: 31g; Total carbs: 261g; Fiber: 23g; Sugar: 78g; Protein: 46g; Sodium: 612mg

Winter Harvest Quinoa Stir-Fry

30-MINUTE, VEGETARIAN

This sweet and savory stir-fry will become one of your go-to meals. Instead of rice, it uses quinoa, which is a complete protein and packs nutrients. Try it with Spicy "Fish" Sauce (page 147).

Serves 4 **Prep time: 5 minutes / Cook time: 25 minutes**

2 cups quinoa, rinsed

2 tablespoons olive oil

1 onion, diced

½ cup peeled and diced sweet potato,

1 cup peeled and diced butternut squash,

2 tablespoons soy sauce

1 egg

1 tablespoon sesame oil

1 cup pomegranate seeds or dried cranberries

1 cup walnuts, chopped

1. In a large pot, bring 3 cups water to a boil. Add the quinoa. Bring it back to a boil, then reduce the heat and cover. Cook on a low simmer for 15 minutes, or until the quinoa is done.

2. In a large skillet, heat the olive oil over medium heat. Add the onion and cook for 3 minutes.

3. Add the sweet potato and butternut squash and cook for 5 minutes. Cover, reduce the heat to low, and cook for 15 minutes more.

4. Once the sweet potato and squash are tender, pour the soy sauce over the stir-fry. Mix well.

5. Push the stir-fry to the edges of the skillet, creating space in the middle. Crack an egg in the space and let cook.

6. Once the egg is cooked, mix it into the stir-fry.

7. Top with sesame oil, pomegranate seeds or dried cranberries, and walnuts.

Prep Tip: Omit the egg to make this recipe vegan.

PER SERVING: Calories: 677; Total fat: 34g; Total carbs: 77g; Fiber: 10g; Sugar: 10g; Protein: 19g; Sodium: 482mg

ORANGE
-POMEGRANATE
SALSA
PAGE 144

chapter six
dressings, sauces, and dips

A sauce can elevate a recipe from everyday to out of this world. This chapter includes pesto, dressings, chutneys, vegan creams, and a "fish" sauce. Add them to wraps, tacos, stir-fries, noodles, or roasted vegetables.

Dairy-Free Caesar Dressing

DAIRY-FREE, 5-INGREDIENT, GLUTEN-FREE, NUT-FREE, 30-MINUTE

Caesar salad is a classic that you can now easily re-create at home.

Serves 2   **Prep time: 7 minutes**

---

1 garlic clove,
  finely chopped
4 anchovies,
  finely chopped
1 egg yolk
1 tablespoon olive oil
1 tablespoon red
  wine vinegar
Pinch salt
Pinch freshly ground
  black pepper

In a small bowl, combine the garlic, anchovies, egg yolk, olive oil, vinegar, salt, and pepper. Using a whisk or fork, mix until well combined.

PER SERVING: Calories: 175; Total fat: 13g; Total carbs: 1g; Fiber: 0g; Sugar: 0g; Protein: 13g; Sodium: 1,539mg

Lemon Tahini

Tahini adds coolness to wraps, falafels, sandwiches, and salads. This tahini gets its kick from cumin and lemon juice. Store in an airtight container in the refrigerator for up to one week.

Serves 2   **Prep time: 5 minutes**

½ cup nondairy yogurt
¼ cup tahini
Juice of 1 lemon
½ teaspoon
  ground cumin
½ teaspoon salt
¼ teaspoon freshly
  ground black pepper

In a blender or food processor, combine the yogurt, tahini, lemon juice, cumin, salt, and pepper. Blend until smooth. (Alternatively, put all the ingredients in a bowl and whisk with a fork.)

PER SERVING: Calories: 222; Total fat: 17g; Total carbs: 14g; Fiber: 3g; Sugar: 5g; Protein: 7g; Sodium: 627mg

Dairy-Free Pesto

DAIRY-FREE, GLUTEN-FREE, NUT-FREE, 30-MINUTE, VEGAN

This pesto is free of common allergens and creamy because it contains avocado. Use it on pastas, salads, and wraps.

Serves 4   **Prep time: 5 minutes**

1 avocado, halved, pitted, and peeled
1 cup fresh basil
1 tablespoon olive oil
Juice of 1 lemon
¼ teaspoon salt
¼ teaspoon freshly ground black pepper

In a blender or food processor, combine the avocado, basil, olive oil, lemon juice, ¼ cup water, salt, and pepper. Blend until smooth.

PER SERVING: Calories: 106; Total fat: 10g; Total carbs: 4g; Fiber: 3g; Sugar: 0g; Protein: 1g; Sodium: 154mg

Spicy Cashew Cheese

5-INGREDIENT, GLUTEN-FREE, 30-MINUTE, VEGAN

This cashew cheese is made with whole ingredients. Try it with noodles, lasagna, burritos, and tacos. If you are not a fan of spice, omit the jalapeño.

Serves 4 **Prep time: 5 minutes**

1 cup raw cashews, soaked
  for 1 hour, drained
2 tablespoons
  nutritional yeast
1 jalapeño
Juice of 1 lemon
½ teaspoon
  yellow mustard
Pinch salt
Pinch freshly ground
  black pepper

In a blender or food processor, combine the drained cashews, nutritional yeast, jalapeño, lemon juice, mustard, salt, and pepper. Blend until smooth.

PER SERVING: Calories: 253; Total fat: 17g; Total carbs: 15g; Fiber: 4g; Sugar: 0g; Protein: 11g; Sodium: 55mg

Orange-Pomegranate Salsa

DAIRY-FREE, 5-INGREDIENT, GLUTEN-FREE, NUT-FREE, 30-MINUTE, VEGAN

This salsa combines sweet, spicy, and sour flavors. The sweetness comes from the pomegranate seeds and orange; the spice, from the jalapeño; and sour, from the lemon. Serve this salsa with chips for dipping.

Serves 4   **Prep time: 15 minutes**

1 orange, peeled and diced

Seeds from 1 pomegranate

Juice of 1 lemon

1 jalapeño, minced

1 tablespoon chopped fresh cilantro

¼ teaspoon salt

¼ teaspoon freshly ground black pepper

1. Put the orange and pomegranate seeds in a bowl. Squeeze the lemon juice over the fruit.

2. Add the jalapeño and cilantro. Season with salt and pepper and toss to combine.

PER SERVING: Calories: 51; Total fat: 0g; Total carbs: 12g; Fiber: 2g; Sugar: 10g; Protein: 1g; Sodium: 14mg

Coconut-Peanut Sauce

DAIRY-FREE, 30-MINUTE, VEGAN

This Southeast Asian–inspired sauce is perfect for noodles, rice, wraps, and spring rolls. Jalapeño adds a little kick.

Serves 4   **Prep time: 5 minutes**

⅓ cup peanut butter

1½ teaspoons curry powder

½ teaspoon coconut oil, melted

2 tablespoons soy sauce

Juice of 1 lemon

2 jalapeños, seeded and finely chopped

1. Put ½ cup water, the peanut butter, curry powder, coconut oil, soy sauce, and lemon juice in a blender or food processor. Blend until smooth.

2. Transfer the sauce to a bowl. Add the jalapeño to the sauce and mix with a fork to combine.

PER SERVING: Calories: 143; Total fat: 12g; Total carbs: 6g; Fiber: 2g; Sugar: 3g; Protein: 6g; Sodium: 553mg

Mango Chutney

A great curry deserves a sweet yet tangy chutney. Try this one with rice dishes, seafood, cheese, and meat.

Serves 6 **Prep time: 5 minutes / Cook time: 20 minutes**

3 cups diced mango
½ cup diced red onion
⅓ cup packed
  brown sugar
3 tablespoons white
  wine vinegar
½ teaspoon salt

1. In a pot, combine the mango, red onion, brown sugar, vinegar, and salt and bring to a boil over medium-high heat. Reduce the heat to maintain a simmer. Simmer for 15 minutes, until thick and syrupy. Remove from the heat.
2. Transfer to a jar and let cool. Store in the refrigerator until ready to use.

PER SERVING: Calories: 86; Total fat: 0g; Total carbs: 21g; Fiber: 2g; Sugar: 19g; Protein: 1g; Sodium: 198mg

Spicy "Fish" Sauce

DAIRY-FREE, 5-INGREDIENT, NUT-FREE, 30-MINUTE, VEGAN

Fish sauce can be hard to find, but it is easy to make at home. This one adds umami flavor without using any animal products. Pair it with fish, meat, or stir-fries.

Serves 5   **Prep time: 5 minutes**

4 tablespoons soy sauce
2 tablespoons brown
  sugar or maple syrup
1 Thai chile, chopped

In a jar, whisk ¼ cup water, the soy sauce, brown sugar, and chile until combined. Refrigerate for up to several months.

PER SERVING: Calories: 21; Total fat: 0g; Total carbs: 4g; Fiber: 0g; Sugar: 4g; Protein: 1g; Sodium: 704mg

Buffalo Sauce

This vegan buffalo sauce doesn't skimp on flavor. Pair it with cauliflower bites, sandwiches, and fries.

Serves 4   **Prep time: 5 minutes**

¼ cup coconut oil, melted
½ cup hot sauce
2 teaspoons apple
   cider vinegar
2 tablespoons paprika

In a small bowl, whisk the coconut oil, hot sauce, vinegar, and paprika until combined.

PER SERVING: Calories: 131; Total fat: 14g; Total carbs: 2g; Fiber: 1g; Sugar: 1g; Protein: 1g; Sodium: 762mg

Dairy-Free Ranch

DAIRY-FREE, 5-INGREDIENT, 30-MINUTE, VEGAN

This rich and tangy ranch dressing gets its sweet note from maple syrup. Use it in salads, wraps, and sandwiches.

Serves 4   **Prep time: 5 minutes / Cook time: 15 minutes**

2 cups raw cashews, soaked in water to cover overnight or boiled for 15 minutes, drained

1 cup unsweetened nondairy milk

3 tablespoons apple cider vinegar

1 teaspoon maple syrup

1 tablespoon freshly squeezed lemon juice

1½ tablespoons minced fresh dill

Pinch salt

Pinch freshly ground black pepper

1. In a blender or food processor, combine the drained cashews, milk, vinegar, maple syrup, lemon juice, dill, salt, and pepper. Blend until smooth.

2. Store in a jar in the refrigerator for up to 2 months.

PER SERVING: Calories: 470; Total fat: 34g; Total carbs: 24g; Fiber: 3g; Sugar: 2g; Protein: 16g; Sodium: 54mg

QUICK REFERENCE GUIDE TO PREPPING AND COOKING VEGETABLES

VEGGIE	PREPPING OPTIONS	TOOLS	RAW/ COOKED	COOK METHODS	SERVING IDEAS
ACORN SQUASH	Slice off stem, halve, remove seeds and pulp; slice into wedges; puree; dice	Chef's knife; spoon; food processor or blender	Cooked	Roast; sauté; steam; braise; slow cooker; pressure cooker	Stuffed roasted halves; roasted wedges; soup
ASPARAGUS	Remove bottom one-third of the stalk, at least, to remove more fibrous ends; peel into ribbons lengthwise; slice into thin disks; puree	Chef's knife; vegetable peeler; food processor or blender	Raw/ cooked	Roast; steam; sauté; simmer; slow cooker; pressure cooker	Salad; add to pasta, legume, grain, and vegetable dishes; soup; pickled; risotto; anything with eggs such as quiche
AVOCADO	Halve lengthwise, twist to separate, remove pit using a knife, slice into wedges, cubes, or chunks, and slide a spoon between the flesh and skin to scoop out; puree; mash	Chef's knife; food processor; mortar and pestle	Raw/ cooked	Grilled, fried	Add to salads, sandwiches, and pasta; guacamole; place wedges on toast and top with olive oil, salt, and pepper; anything with cooked eggs such as omelets; add to smoothie; use in a sauce or dressing
BASIL, MINT, SAGE	Roll or stack to thinly slice; mash using a mortar and pestle; puree	Chef's knife; food processor; mortar and pestle	Raw/ cooked	Sauté; roast; simmer	Pesto; add to salads, vegetables, grains, legumes, pasta, and eggs; add to dressings and sauces; add to pizza and breads such as focaccia

VEGGIE	PREPPING OPTIONS	TOOLS	RAW/COOKED	COOK METHODS	SERVING IDEAS
BEETS	Slice off ends and peel; chop; dice; spiralize red beets; purée; peel into ribbons; grate	Chef's knife; paring knife; vegetable peeler; spiralizer; food processor or blender; box grater	Raw/cooked	Sauté; roast; simmer; steam; bake; slow cooker; pressure cooker	Chilled soup with sour cream and dill; pickle; add to salads, pasta, grains, and vegetable dishes; add purée to breads or chocolate cake batter, ravioli filling, or pasta dough; add spiralized noodles to soups or use as pasta noodles; bake as chips; raw slaws; sauté with butter and maple syrup
BELL PEPPERS	Place a pepper on a workspace with the stem facing up, and slice the side "lobes" off, slice off the bottom, discard the seeds, pith, and top (which should be all connected as one piece); slice into lengths; dice; puree	Chef's knife; food processor or blender	Raw/cooked	Roast; sauté; simmer; bake; grill; stir-fry; slow cooker; pressure cooker	Roast and peel, halve, seed, and drizzle with olive oil, plus capers, garlic, salt, and pepper; pureed soup; add to tomato sauces; stuff whole with grains and vegetables; add to salads, sandwiches, grains, legumes, and pasta; appetizer with a dip; add to bread; add to a sofrito of onion, celery, and carrots; add to sauces such as aioli
BOK CHOY	Slice off root end and use whole or chop	Chef's knife	Raw/cooked	Braise; grill; sauté; simmer; roast; stir-fry; steam	Warm or raw salad; raw slaws; soup; ramen; add to grains, vegetables, and legume dishes; raw with a dip for an appetizer; pickled; add to a green smoothie

VEGGIE	PREPPING OPTIONS	TOOLS	RAW/COOKED	COOK METHODS	SERVING IDEAS
BROCCOLI	Trim fibrous ends and snap off leaves; peel off the outer tough skin; separate florets by slicing through the stems; slice the stems into batons, thinly slice into disks, chop, or dice; use florets and stem; puree	Chef's knife; food processor or blender; food mill (for removing seed pods from a puree)	Raw/cooked	Bake; blanch; braise; fry; grill; roast; sauté; simmer; steam; stir-fry; slow cooker; pressure cooker	Add to egg dishes such as casseroles and quiche; roast with olive oil, smoky paprika, salt, and pepper, and finish with lemon juice; stir-fry with other vegetables in sesame oil, and finish with soy sauce; add to raw salads, Buddha bowls, grains, legumes, and vegetable casseroles; roast and toss with pasta, capers, preserved lemon, grated Parmesan cheese, and toasted bread crumbs; soup; add roasted broccoli to pizza toppings
BRUSSELS SPROUTS	Trim bottoms and remove any wilted or yellowed leaves; thinly slice; halve	Chef's knife; food processor fitted with a grater	Raw/cooked	Roast; bake; steam; braise; fry; sauté; grill; pressure cooker; slow cooker	Slice thinly for a raw salad with scallions and dried cranberries; roast with apples; make a hash with potatoes, onion, and apple cider vinegar; toss with garlic, spices, and olive oil, and throw on the grill; bake into a cheesy gratin
BUTTERNUT SQUASH	Slice off ends, cut the squash in two just above the bulbous end, stand on end and peel with a sharp knife or vegetable peeler; scoop out seeds with a spoon; slice into wedges; chop; dice; puree; spiralize	Chef's knife; food processor; blender; spiralizer	Cooked	Roast; sauté; steam; simmer; slow cooker; pressure cooker	Stuff with grains and/or vegetables; spiralize into pasta; add to salads, grains, legumes, and vegetables; soup; risotto
CABBAGE	Slice into wedges; thinly slice; grate	Chef's knife; box grater	Raw/cooked	Roast; braise; sauté; steam; grill; bake; stir-fry; slow cooker	Roast wedges rubbed with olive oil, garlic paste, salt, and pepper; braise red cabbage with olive oil, cider vinegar, brown sugar, and apple chunks; slaw; cabbage rolls stuffed with rice and vegetables; pickle for kimchi; topping for tacos; make colcannon with potatoes

VEGGIE	PREPPING OPTIONS	TOOLS	RAW/ COOKED	COOK METHODS	SERVING IDEAS
CARROT	Trim top, and peel; slice; dice; grate; peel into ribbons	Chef's knife; paring knife; box grater; vegetable peeler	Raw/ cooked	Roast; braise; sauté; steam; grill; bake; stir-fry; slow cooker; pressure cooker; simmer; steam	Raw salad; soup; slaw; soufflé; bread; cake; add to vegetable, grain, and legume dishes; simmer in a pan with butter, honey, and orange juice until all the liquid is gone except a glaze
CAULIFLOWER	Trim bottom and remove leaves; slice into steaks; cut off florets at the stems; chop or dice stems; grate into rice; puree; mash	Chef's knife; paring knife; box grater; food processor or blender	Raw/ cooked	Bake; blanch; braise; fry; grill; roast; sauté; simmer; steam; stir-fry; pressure cooker; slow cooker	Puree into a sauce; grate into rice for tabbouleh or risotto; roast whole, smothered with a spicy sauce; substitute it for chicken in many dishes; soup; pickle for kimchi; swap out potatoes in mashed potatoes; use in a gratin; toss with pasta, lemon, capers, and bread crumbs
CELERY	Trim bottoms; slice into long strips; dice	Chef's knife	Raw/ cooked	Roast; braise; sauté; bake; stir-fry; simmer	Use for making stock; sofrito; make a celery gratin; braise in broth with tomatoes, onions, and top with shavings of Parmesan; add to salads for crunch
CORN	Remove kernels by standing a cob up in a bowl lined with a towel. Anchor it with one hand, and slide a knife down the cob to slice off the kernels. Slide the knife down a second time to harvest corn milk.	Chef's knife	Raw/ cooked	Sauté; roast; simmer; steam; grill	Chowder; stew; add to tacos with black beans, tomatoes, and avocado with a squeeze of lime; sauté with pickled onion, basil, and tomatoes and stuff into peppers with a little cheese; risotto; toss with zoodles, mint, and tomatoes; make Mexican corn
CUCUMBER	Peel, halve, and scrape out juicy seeds; slice into thin or thick slices; peel into long ribbons; dice; grate; pickle	Vegetable peeler; chef's knife; paring knife; spoon; box grater	Raw/ cooked	Sauté; bake; stir-fry	Use in salads, especially Greek- and Middle Eastern-inspired salads; make tzatziki; swap out bread for cucumber disks; pickles; chilled soup; make a sandwich with cream cheese and dill; add slices to jugs of water; sauté with a little butter, salt, pepper, scallions, and mint

VEGGIE	PREPPING OPTIONS	TOOLS	RAW/COOKED	COOK METHODS	SERVING IDEAS
DELICATA SQUASH	Slice off the ends, halve, and scrape out the seeds; slice into half-moons; puree	Chef's knife; spoon; food processor or blender	Cooked	Roast; bake; sauté; simmer; grill; braise; steam; slow cooker; pressure cooker; stir-fry	Soup; stuff scooped-out half with grains, dried fruits, and other vegetables; drizzle with oil and garlic, sprinkle with salt, pepper, and cayenne, and roast; add to warm salads or Buddha bowls; use as a pizza topping; toss with pasta; add to tacos; puree to add to chilis and stews; bake into a gratin
EGGPLANT	Slice off the ends, slice into ¾-inch slices, sprinkle evenly with salt, and lay in a colander to drain for 30 minutes. Rinse to remove the salt, and dry. Use as slices, or chop, dice, mash, or puree	Chef's knife; colander	Cooked	Bake; roast; sauté; simmer; grill; stir-fry; braise; slow cooker; pressure cooker	Mash into a dip such as baba ghanoush; marinate and grill for a sandwich with tomatoes and smoked mozzarella; lightly bread and bake in a tomato sauce topped with Parmesan; roast and stuff with a grain and pomegranate seed salad; simmer with tomatoes, onion, garlic, and balsamic vinegar and puree for a soup
GARLIC	Chop; thinly slice; mince; smash and lightly salt to form a paste	Chef's knife	Raw/cooked	Roast; sauté; blanch; bake; stir-fry	Wrap a head of garlic with a drizzle of olive oil and a sprig of rosemary in foil and roast; sauté or roast chopped or thinly sliced garlic with vegetables, legumes, or grains; soup with onions and thyme
GINGER	Peel with a spoon and trim; slice; mince; grate	Spoon; paring knife; fine grater or zester	Raw/cooked	Simmer; sauté; stir-fry	Tea; add to broths and soups; grate finely to add to fruit with a squeeze of fresh lime; add to miso and garlic paste to rub on vegetables; gingerbread; add to sauces or jams
GREEN BEANS	Trim; slice lengthwise; slice crosswise on the diagonal	Paring knife or chef's knife	Cooked	Blanch; sauté; simmer; bake; roast; stir-fry	Add to salads, soups, and grains; roast with olive oil, thyme, salt, pepper, and a squeeze of lemon

VEGGIE	PREPPING OPTIONS	TOOLS	RAW/ COOKED	COOK METHODS	SERVING IDEAS
JALAPEÑO PEPPERS, SERRANO PEPPERS	Trim off the stem, halve, and remove the seeds and pith; slice; dice; mince	Paring knife	Raw/ cooked	Sauté; roast; bake; stir-fry	Roast with corn bread batter; roast with cheese; add to vegetable and legume dishes; pickle; add to cheese sandwiches or quesadillas; traditional tomato salsas or with diced pineapple and mango; jelly
KALE	Fold leaves over the central tough rib and remove the rib with a knife (not necessary for baby kale); coarsely chop	Chef's knife	Raw/ cooked	Sauté; blanch; bake; roast; stir-fry; simmer; braise; grill; steam	Pesto; baked kale chips; sauté with lemon, olives, and capers, and toss with quinoa; add to soup; braise with garlic, dried chipotle chiles, and tomatoes; add to a green smoothie
LEEKS	Cut and discard the top part of the leek with tough, dark green leaves, split in half lengthwise, and feather under cold running water; slice into thin half-moons	Chef's knife	Raw/ cooked	Sauté; roast	Add to sautéed or roasted vegetables; roast halves in the oven with olive oil, salt, and pepper; raw in salads
MUSHROOMS, SMALL	Wipe clean with a paper towel, and slice, quarter, or mince.	Chef's knife	Raw/ cooked	Sauté; bake; stir-fry; roast; braise; grill	Coat with olive oil and a dusting of salt and pepper and roast at 400°F until well browned; add to pasta and grains dishes; make mushroom risotto; stuff with peppers, garlic, bread crumbs, and Parmesan cheese for an appetizer; use in casseroles
OLIVES (GREEN, NIÇOISE, KALAMATA)	Slice; smash using the flat side of a chef's knife; coarsely chopped; left whole	Chef's knife	Raw/ cooked	Sauté; roast	Add to pastas, grains, vegetables, and legumes
ONIONS, SHALLOTS	Chop; dice; grate; slice	Chef's knife	Raw/ cooked	Bake; braise; fry; grill; roast; sauté; stir-fry; pressure cooker; slow cooker	Stuff sweet onions with grains and other vegetables and roast; caramelize and add to sandwiches, burgers, grains, and legumes; make a flatbread with caramelized onions, ricotta cheese, and herbs
PARSLEY AND CILANTRO	Hold a sharp knife at a 45-degree angle to the herbs and slice across the leaves to coarsely chop, including stems; gather the leaves and stems together and chop into smaller pieces; or continue chopping to mince	Chef's knife	Raw/ cooked	Suitable for all kinds of cooking	Add to most vegetable, pasta, grain, and legume dishes, including roasts, soups, and casseroles.

VEGGIE	PREPPING OPTIONS	TOOLS	RAW/COOKED	COOK METHODS	SERVING IDEAS
PEAS	Pry the shells open with your nails or a small knife and remove the peas; puree	Food processor or blender	Raw/cooked	Bake; blanch; braise; sauté; simmer; steam; stir-fry	Add to pasta, casseroles, soup, and vegetable dishes; puree for a pea soup; lightly sauté with salt and pepper, and toss with mint; add to an asparagus quiche or omelet
PORTABELLA MUSHROOMS	Wipe clean with a paper towel, and scrape out the gills using a spoon; leave whole or slice	Chef's knife; spoon	Raw/cooked	Grill; roast; sauté; braise; bake; braise	Use in place of a bun for veggie burgers; stuff with vegetables, grains, or legumes; marinate in olive oil, balsamic vinegar, and garlic and roast or grill
POTATOES (WHITE, RED, YUKON GOLD, FINGERLING)	Peel; slice; dice; mash; puree; grate; spiralize; smash	Vegetable peeler; chef's knife; paring knife; potato ricer or masher; box grater; spiralizer; food processor (using pulse only)	Cooked	Bake; braise; fry; grill; pressure cooker; roast; sauté; simmer; slow cooker; steam; stir-fry	Twice-baked potatoes whipped with soft cheese topped with chives; shoestring fries using the spiralizer, tossed with olive oil, salt, and pepper, and roasted until brown; grilled slices of potato to add to salads; potato gratin; smash roasted baby red potatoes, sprinkle with salt, pepper, and dried rosemary, and drizzle with olive oil
RADISHES	Trim roots and tops; leave whole, halve, or thinly slice	Paring knife	Raw/cooked	Bake; braise; fry; stir-fry	Bake or roast with butter, salt, pepper, and parsley; add to salads
SCALLIONS (GREEN ONIONS)	Trim roots and remove any outer damaged sheath; leave whole, halve lengthwise, or chop	Paring knife or chef's knife	Raw/cooked	Braise; roast; grill; sauté; stir-fry	Toss in olive oil, salt and pepper and roast or grill; pickle; add to salads, soups, pasta, grains, pizza, or legume dishes; add to any kind of egg dishes
SPAGHETTI SQUASH	Halve or leave whole; scoop out seeds and pulp; after cooking, run the tines of a fork across the flesh to pull up spaghetti strands	Chef's knife; spoon; fork	Cooked	Roast; bake; pressure cook; slow cook	Stuff with black beans, roasted red peppers, and onions, and top with cheese; toss strands with olive oil, Parmesan cheese, salt, pepper, and roasted pumpkin seeds
SPINACH	Stack leaves, remove stems, roll into a fat cigar shape, and thinly slice; gather slices together and mince	Chef's knife	Raw/cooked	Blanch; braise; sauté; simmer; stir-fry	Sauté in a little olive oil, salt and, pepper, and toss with cooked quinoa, yellow raisins, and a squeeze of lemon; add to soups, salads, sandwiches, and pasta; mince for spanakopita

VEGGIE	PREPPING OPTIONS	TOOLS	RAW/ COOKED	COOK METHODS	SERVING IDEAS
SUGAR SNAP PEAS, SNOW PEAS	Trim ends and leave whole or thinly slice	Paring knife or chef's knife	Raw/ cooked	Bake; braise; grill; roast; sauté; steam; stir-fry	Toss in olive oil, salt, and pepper and grill, and toss with chopped mint before serving; sauté and sprinkle with Maldon sea salt; sauté in sesame oil, and finish with lemon, salt, pepper, and sesame seeds
SWEET POTATOES	Peel with a vegetable peeler; slice; dice; chop; grate; spiralize; puree	Chef's knife; vegetable peeler; spiralizer; food processor or blender; box grater	Cooked	Roast; bake; sauté; simmer; grill; steam; slow cooker; pressure cooker	Baked and stuffed; spiralized pasta; puree for a sauce, soup or to add to pancake batter; add to stews and chili; enchiladas; tacos; season, roast, and add to warm salads and Buddha bowls; add to root vegetable roasts and gratins; baked sweet potato chips; sauté with butter and maple syrup; season and bake sweet potato fries; hash
SWISS CHARD, MUSTARD GREENS, DANDELION GREENS	Remove the central fibrous stem, if applicable, and stack several leaves on top of each other. Fold in half lengthwise, and roll into a fat cigar shape. Slice crosswise into wide or narrow ribbons. Gather ribbons together and finely chop or mince.	Chef's knife	Raw/ cooked	Bake; blanch; braise; roast; sauté; simmer; steam	Use Swiss chard leaves for rolling up grains and vegetables, cover with a pasta sauce and cheese, and bake; sauté Swiss chard stems separately with garlic, salt, and pepper, finished with a vinegar drizzle; sauté garlic and onion, add broth, salt, and pepper, and braise mustard greens until tender; sauté dandelion greens in olive oil, garlic, salt, black pepper, and red pepper flakes

VEGGIE	PREPPING OPTIONS	TOOLS	RAW/ COOKED	COOK METHODS	SERVING IDEAS
TOMATOES	To peel a tomato, score the skin on the bottom of the tomato with an "X," blanch in simmering water for 20 seconds, followed by a dip in a bowl of ice water, and peel starting at the "X"; slice, chop or dice; grate; puree	Paring knife or chef's knife; box grater; food processor or blender	Raw/ cooked	Bake; blanch; braise; fry; grill; roast; sauté; simmer; stir-fry	Stuff raw with chickpea or lentil salad; slice in half and slow-roast with garlic, salt, and pepper; panzanella (bread salad); tomato jam; salsa; caprese bruschetta; gazpacho
ZUCCHINI, SUMMER SQUASH	Trim the ends and chop, dice, or slice into rounds, wedges, or matchstick lengths; grate using the largest holes of a box grater; spiralize	Paring knife or chef's knife; box grater; spiralizer; food processor or blender	Raw/ cooked	Bake; grill; roast; sauté; simmer; steam; stir-fry	Bake as fries: slice into wedges, toss in olive oil, salt, pepper, oregano, and Parmesan cheese; spiralize for spaghetti toss with tomatoes, basil, and garlic; slice in half lengthwise and slightly hollow out to make boats for stuffing vegetables and grains, topped with pasta sauce and cheese

MEASUREMENT CONVERSIONS

VOLUME EQUIVALENTS (LIQUID)

US Standard (ounces)	US Standard (approximate)	Metric
2 tablespoons	1 fl.oz.	30 mL
¼ cup	2 fl. oz.	60 mL
½ cup	4 fl. oz.	120 mL
1 cup	8 fl. oz.	240 mL
1½ cups	12 fl.oz.	355 mL
2 cups or 1 pint	16 fl. oz.	475 mL
4 cups or 1 quart	32 fl. oz.	1 L
1 gallon	128 fl.oz.	4 L

OVEN TEMPERATURES

Fahrenheit (F)	Celsius (C) (approximate)
250°F	120°C
300°F	150°C
325°F	165°C
350°F	180°C
375°F	190°C
400°F	200°C
425°F	220°C
450°F	230°C

VOLUME EQUIVALENTS (DRY)

US Standard	Metric (approximate)
⅛ teaspoon	0.5 mL
¼ teaspoon	1 mL
½ teaspoon	2 mL
¾ teaspoon	4 mL
1 teaspoon	5 mL
1 tablespoon	15 mL
¼ cup	60 mL
⅓ cup	79 mL
½ cup	120 mL
⅔ cup	156 mL
¾ cup	177 mL
1 cup	240 mL
2 cups or 1 pint	475 mL
3 cups	700 mL
4 cups or 1 quart	1 L

WEIGHT EQUIVALENTS

US Standard	Metric (approximate)
½ ounce	15 g
1 ounce	30 g
2 ounces	60 g
4 ounces	115 g
8 ounces	225 g
12 ounces	340 g
16 ounces or 1 pound	455 g

RECIPE MEAL TYPE INDEX

Dinner

INDEX

ACKNOWLEDGMENTS

I would like to thank my partner, Jared, for being the wonderful dog dad that he is to our two rescue pit bulls, Ladybird and Shelby, and to our cat, Desmond. Thank you for being my biggest fan, for your patience and support, and for holding it down while I isolated from the world to study and write this book.

I'd also like to send thanks to my sister, Renata, and best friend, Mischa, for providing a lot of laughter in person, on the phone, and on the thread during stressful times. Laughter really is the best medicine.

I would also like to send gratitude to those who are actively bettering our planet and to those who are bringing awareness to animal welfare and helping animals in need.

Lastly, thank you to the wonderful publishing team at Callisto Media for putting this project together! It has been wonderful working with everyone, and I am so grateful for this publishing opportunity!

ABOUT THE AUTHOR

Larissa Olczak has been a vegetarian/vegan for 15 years. A graduate of California State University, Northridge, she is a nutritional therapy practitioner and certified herbalist who studied at the Dandelion Herbal Center and the Herbal Academy. She is also a health and wellness blogger and a recipe developer. Larissa helps people create healthy relationships with food by providing education on holistic wellness, healthy lifestyles, and delicious vegan recipes. She is from Oakland, California, where she lives with her boyfriend, two rescue dogs, and a cat.